MIND THE GAPS

Singapore Business in China

The **Institute of Southeast Asian Studies (ISEAS)** was established as an autonomous organization in 1968. It is a regional centre dedicated to the study of socio-political, security and economic trends and developments in Southeast Asia and its wider geostrategic and economic environment.

The Institute's research programmes are the Regional Economic Studies (RES, including ASEAN and APEC), Regional Strategic and Political Studies (RSPS), and Regional Social and Cultural Studies (RSCS).

ISEAS Publications, an established academic press, has issued more than 1,000 books and journals. It is the largest scholarly publisher of research about Southeast Asia from within the region. ISEAS Publications works with many other academic and trade publishers and distributors to disseminate important research and analyses from and about Southeast Asia to the rest of the world.

MIND THE GAPS

Singapore Business in China

Sree Kumar
Sharon Siddique
Yuwa Hedrick-Wong

ISEAS INSTITUTE OF SOUTHEAST ASIAN STUDIES
Singapore

First published in Singapore in 2005 by ISEAS Publications
Institute of Southeast Asian Studies
30 Heng Mui Keng Terrace
Pasir Panjang
Singapore 119614

E-mail: publish@iseas.edu.sg
Website: <http://bookshop.iseas.edu.sg>

The responsibility for facts and opinions in this publication rests exclusively with the authors and their interpretations do not necessarily reflect the views or the policy of the publisher or its supporters.

ISEAS Library Cataloguing-in-Publication Data

Mind the gaps : Singapore business in China / Sree Kumar, Sharon Siddique, Yuwa Hedrick-Wong.
1. Investments, Singapore—China.
2. Corporate culture—Singapore.
3. Corporate culture—China.
4. Singapore—Commerce—China.
5. China—Commerce—Singapore.
6. Singapore—Foreign economic relations—China.
7. China—Foreign economic relations—Singapore.
I. Title
II. Singapore business in China
III. Siddique, Sharon.
IV. Wong, Yuwa Hedrick.
HF1595 Z4C5S77   2005

ISBN 981-230-267-0 (soft cover)
ISBN 981-230-274-3 (hard cover)

Typeset by Superskill Graphics Pte Ltd
Printed in Singapore by

Contents

Foreword

China, the new economic powerhouse of Asia, burst onto the world stage in the mid-80s, and has been able to sustain rapid growth for the past two decades, defying even the most optimistic forecasts. China has transformed itself into an attractive designation for foreign direct investments to fuel its economic expansion. Foreign investors have brought fresh capital, advanced technology and management know-how to tap business opportunities in all the different sectors.

Many Singaporean businessmen and corporations have extensive engagement with their Chinese counterparts and some were amongst the early business entrants into China. Though there are many opportunities available, we did not fully capitalize on our early mover's advantage and the numerous initiatives/incentives introduced by our government agencies. Generally, there still exist considerable gaps for Singapore business to do well in China.

This publication offers a useful framework for understanding the gaps of Singapore business in the dynamic business landscape of China. It gives a holistic outlook of Singapore business in China derived from the invaluable experiences of many of our industry veterans operating in China as well as the frank perspectives provided by our Chinese and foreign counterparts.

The Singapore Business Federation and its member chambers have played an important role in increasing the awareness of market opportunities, operational pitfalls and the soft side of conducting business in China. Apart from working closely with the different government agencies that encourage our businessmen and corporations to venture overseas, the Singapore business community will also have to find ways for corporations to collaborate more, in order to shorten the learning curve and to mitigate the risks of going into China. We should pool our capabilities together to surmount many of the gaps of individual companies.

Some Singaporeans on their own have managed to bridge the gaps of conducting businesses in China and made their marks in different parts of the country. The inroads made by these successful forerunners in business are useful in guiding other Singaporeans to venture into China.

In this respect I congratulate the authors of the book for their study, which provides deep personal insights into the dynamics of doing business in China and the evolving business relationships with China.

Stephen Lee
Chairman
Singapore Business Federation

Preface

Mind the Gaps: Singapore Business in China is the result of a six-month study completed in June 2004, which explored various dimensions of the Singapore business experience in China. The high priority given to entering the China market reflects a general consensus that "getting it right" in China is one of the most important positioning exercises for Singapore's success in the 21st century. But there is also a general acknowledgement that "the winning formula" has yet to be perfected. The study is based on two types of data. First, quantitative, comparative data charting the contemporary history of Singapore's rapidly accelerating China trajectory was collected and analysed. Second, interviews were conducted with businessmen, bureaucrats, and academics in Singapore and China.

The authors worked closely with a team from the Chinese Marketing Research Centre of Fudan University who managed the China portion of the study. Interviews in China were conducted in Shanghai, Liaoning, and Zhejiang provinces — chosen because of Singapore's extensive existing involvement, and current focus on expanding business relationships. We interviewed a total of 88 business executives, bureaucrats, and academics in China and Singapore, including 48 Chinese nationals (including 3 from Taiwan), 38 Singaporeans, and 2 Chinese Malaysians.

The purpose of these interviews was to understand Mainland Chinese views on Singapore businesses operating in China, and Singapore views on doing business in China. Interviews were conducted either in Mandarin or in English, and the working language of analysis is English. There was no formal questionnaire, and no attempt was made to quantify interviewee responses, other than to note how frequently a particular observation was recorded. (For details on the interviews, see Appendix 1.)

The first chapter of the report traces policy milestones and compiles quantitative, comparative data charting the contemporary history of

Singapore's rapidly accelerating China trajectory. But these growth statistics also highlight an increasing asymmetry. Singapore is more dependent on China than China is on Singapore. One way for Singapore to manage this asymmetry is to target emerging provinces and cities, and carve out a niche as a more significant player through building networks of provincial and city government and business relations. Proceeding from macroeconomic data to the firm level, it is possible to describe the Singapore experience in more detail.

The second chapter draws largely on our interviews with Singapore and China business players, and analyses their observations and insights on Singapore's business operations in China. Cultural perceptions are illustrated through business management, operational styles, and business practices. In the rapidly expanding constellation of foreign business entrants into China, Singapore occupies a distinct, and unique position. What gradually emerged out of analysing these interviews is a collective narrative on Singapore-China business relations.

Particularly in the past decade, China has seen the arrival of more foreign businessmen than at any time in recent history. China is grappling with how to categorize this new constellation of foreigners, and also how to process this interaction in their business dealings. Narrowing our focus, there emerges a narrative on what specifically distinguishes Mainland Chinese from Singapore businessmen, and what makes them unique. Thus beyond what the numbers tell us, and what various government policies attempt to foster, one needs to mark what people say.

The final chapter draws on the research findings of the previous chapters, and distills some of the more important lessons learnt from the Singapore experience in China. This includes an analysis and assessment of current and future trends relevant to successful business positioning in China, and options for Singapore entrepreneurs. Singapore's business investments in China can be viewed collectively as an attempt to transfer business models that have been successful in Singapore, into the Chinese business environment.

For Singapore transfers to succeed, ideally, the operating environment should be similar. If it is not, then the Singapore model must be adapted to fit the new set of circumstances. This adaptation process requires a culturally sensitive implementation capability. Singapore's investments in China present a complex picture, and the learning curve has been steep. The impression is that there are more successful ventures now than previously, as Singapore business people become more savvy, more experienced, and more knowledgeable about China.

Special thanks to the businessmen, bureaucrats and academics in Singapore and China who so generously offered us their time and shared their experiences. Our thanks go to members of our research team. Ms Lee Yew Ying and Ms Parhana Moreta assisted in data collection, analysis, and arranging and conducting interviews in Singapore. Professor Lu Xiongwen and his very capable research team at the Chinese Marketing Research Center of Fudan University, China provided their invaluable assistance with data collection and interviews in Shanghai, Liaoning and Zhejiang.

We would also like to record our appreciation to ISEAS for supporting this research project. We would like to thank Mr K. Kesavapany, ISEAS Director, who has given us encouragement and useful feedback. We are also indebted to the ISEAS research staff for organizing and attending the work-in-progress seminars to review project milestones. Our thanks also to the ISEAS Publications Unit, and particularly, Mrs Triena Ong, Managing Editor, for her usual professionalism transforming a manuscript into a monograph. Finally, we, as authors, take full responsibility for the interpretations and conclusions presented in this study.

About the Authors

SREE KUMAR is a Director of Sreekumar Siddique & Co, an international research and consulting firm. In his varied career, he has been a development economist, management consultant, design engineer, R&D manager, and geophysical engineer in the oil and gas industry. In recent years he has specialized in policy design for governments, public sector reforms, trade and financial sector strategies, and in turning around state-owned enterprises. Sree has a multi-disciplinary background which includes an LLB (Hons) from the University of London; an M.Sc. in Development Economics from Oxford University; an MBA from the Cranfield School of Management; a BSc (Hons) in Economics from the University of London; and a BEng. in Electrical Engineering from the University of Singapore. He was previously a Fellow of the Institute of Southeast Asian Studies in Singapore (1990–94).

SHARON SIDDIQUE is a Director of Sreekumar Siddique & Co, an international research and consulting firm. She monitors regional development, politics, demographic and social trends, and brings a wider perspective to traditional methods of quantitative analysis. She is a leading expert on ethnicity, cross-cultural studies, and religion, and has published extensively on Islam in the Asia-Pacific. Sharon began her interest in cultural studies via languages, earning a BA degree in Linguistics (German and Spanish) from the University of Montana in the USA. After coming to Singapore in the late 1960s, she enrolled in the MA programme in Malay Studies at the University of Singapore. In the early 1970s she lived in Jakarta, where she did extensive fieldwork on culture and religion. She completed her Ph.D. in Development Sociology at the University of Bielefeld, in Germany. She was previously the Deputy Director of the Institute of Southeast Asian Studies (1990–94).

YUWA HEDRICK-WONG is Economic Advisor to MasterCard in Asia. He is a frequent commentator on CNBC and the BBC on current economic issues in the Asia Pacific, a visiting professor at the Chicago Business School in Singapore, and a published author on economic development and international relations. Yuwa gained his field experience in the early 1980s in Japan and China, and subsequently worked in Europe, Sub-Sahara Africa, and the South Pacific. For the past 12 years, he has focused on the Asia Pacific region, concentrating specifically on areas of economic fundamentals and business strategies. Yuwa studied philosophy, political science and economics at Trent University, Ontario, Canada; and pursued post-graduate training in economics at Simon Fraser University and the University of British Columbia in Vancouver, where he received his Ph.D.

1

Singapore's China Trajectory

Introduction

China has become an important manufacturing base in the global production network, producing consumer goods, electronics, technology-intensive products and low-value added merchandise such as garments, textiles, leather goods and the like. This importance and position in the global economy began in the early 1990s and has grown at an incredibly rapid pace.[1] In the last decade, economic growth in China averaged 8.7 per cent per year.[2] In 2003, China's GDP stood at US$1,400 billion, a 9.1 per cent growth over the previous year. This significant growth and accompanying development, as the country opened up, became a magnet for investments of other kinds as well. These other investments have included real estate, finance and business services, and those in the leisure and travel industry, among others.

China is now both a substantial market and an investment location that cannot be ignored. It competes with low-wage manufacturing locations in the rest of Asia, directly, and with other locations outside Asia, indirectly. Singapore has, from the early days of China's open-door

FIGURE 1.1
China Gross Domestic Product 1970–2002

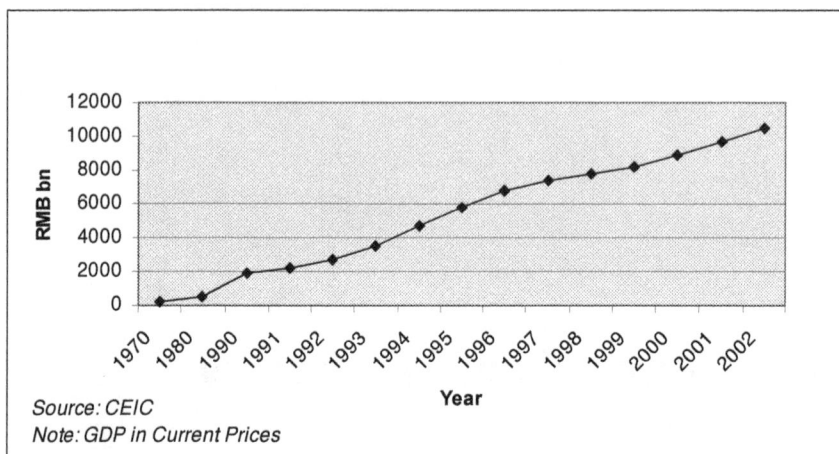

Source: CEIC
Note: GDP in Current Prices

policy, been an interested participant in China's development and progress. In the initial stages of the open-door policy, investments from Singapore were mainly small, family-oriented ventures seeking out opportunities in their ancestral villages or towns. This was the period of the "great discovery" of family roots after the closure of China following the Cultural Revolution in the 1960s.[3]

The serious and larger-scale investments into China from Singapore came about after diplomatic relations were established between the two countries in 1990. The early 1990s saw Singapore place greater emphasis on regional expansion of its economic space, there being a need to seek better opportunities in the emerging markets of Asia. China was one of the promising markets that appeared on the horizon at that time. One of the largest investments from Singapore then was the Suzhou Industrial Park, begun in 1994. This was followed by several investments by government-linked companies (GLCs) which began to export the Singapore development model to China.[4] These included industrial and business parks, modelled on Jurong Town Corporation (JTC); ports and logistics infrastructure, modelled on the Port of Singapore Authority (PSA); and hotel, housing, and leisure construction, modelled on the Housing and

Development Board (HDB), JTC, Sembawang Corporation, Keppel Corporation, and CapitaLand.

In parallel with this thrust went government statutory boards such as International Enterprise (IE) Singapore, SPRING (Standards, Productivity and Innovation Board) Singapore, the Economic Development Board (EDB), and investment agencies such as Temasek Holdings to develop an overall investment strategy into China, and to assist Singapore companies that were part of the strategy. A more recent element of that game plan has been to disseminate information on, and encourage investments in, provinces that did not enjoy the initial benefits of China's opening up. These other coastal provinces such as Liaoning, in the north, and Zhejiang, south of Shanghai, have become important in their own right as industrial development has spread across the coastal region of China. There are other inland provinces which are now of interest to investors as these become part of the changing development landscape in China. Singapore has taken a significant interest in the investment opportunities becoming available in Liaoning and Zhejiang.

OVERVIEW OF SINGAPORE INVESTMENTS AND TRADE IN CHINA

Singapore-China Investments

In the last decade Singapore has been actively promoting investments in China. Between 1992 and 2001, Singapore investments in China grew at a CAGR (compound annual growth rate) of around 53 per cent. In 1997 China became Singapore's top foreign investment destination, accounting for just under 14 per cent of Singapore's total investments abroad as shown in Table 1.1. This proportion then increased to 17.6 per cent in 1998 before declining slightly in the following years.

Most of Singapore's investments in China are in manufacturing and real estate.[5] As shown in Table 1.2, in 2001, of some S$16.5 billion invested in China, about 63 per cent was in manufacturing and just over 17 per cent in real estate. By the end of 2002, Singapore had over US$24.3 billion invested in over 11,800 projects in China.[6] Between January and June of 2002, for example, Singapore invested in over 400 projects in China, with a total contractual value of US$1.9 billion, an increase of 132 per cent over the same period the previous year.[7]

TABLE 1.1
Singapore's Total Direct Investment in China, 1985, 1995–2001

Year	% Share
1985	2.6
1995	7.9
1996	12.0
1997	13.9
1998	17.6
1999	16.9
2000	16.8
2001	12.3

Note: Investments are Direct Equity Investments
Source: CEIC

TABLE 1.2
Structure of Singapore Investments in China, 1997, 2000, 2001

Year	Total direct investment (S$ million)	% Distribution by Activity within China				
		Manu-facturing	Commerce	Financial	Real Estate	Business Services
1997	10,477	60.0	5.5	3.0	21.0	1.0
2000	15,710	63.6	5.3	3.9	17.3	0.8
2001	16,543	62.6	5.7	4.7	17.4	0.6

Source: Department of Statistics, Singapore.

Singapore's investments in China have also fluctuated over the last fifteen years as the effects of the Asian financial crisis spread across the region. Singapore investments as a percentage of China's total FDI have ranged from 3.5 per cent in 1994 to a high of 7.5 per cent in 1998 before declining to just over 4 per cent in 2002. The rates of growth of investment over the last decade, however, have been volatile as shown in Figure 1.2. Between 1995 and 1997 the rate of growth of investments in China from Singapore declined from over 50 per cent to below 20 per

FIGURE 1.2
Growth of Singapore Investments in China, 1994–2002

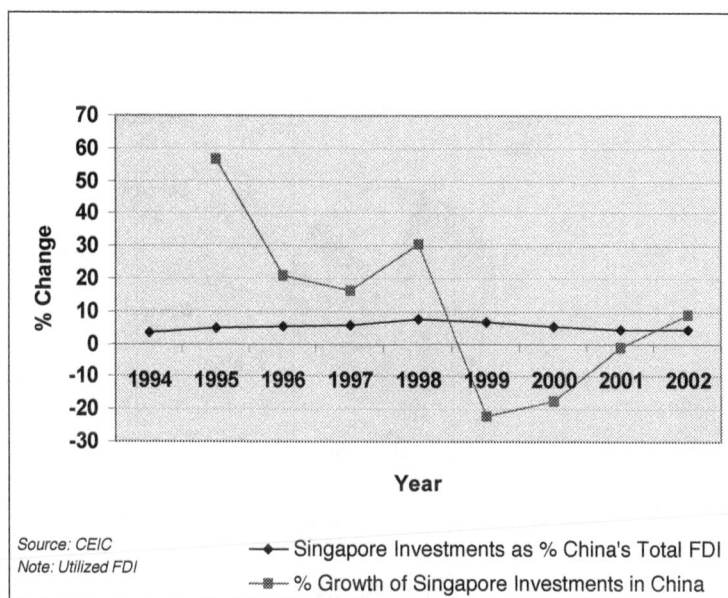

Source: CEIC
Note: Utilized FDI

──◆── Singapore Investments as % China's Total FDI
──■── % Growth of Singapore Investments in China

cent and then increased to 30 per cent before falling sharply to a negative 20 per cent in 1999. Since then there has been a gradual increase to about 10 per cent in 2002.

While the Singapore-China investment profile shows large swings, it is important to place it in the larger perspective of China's overall investment structure. As seen in Figure 1.3 the largest investor in China is Hong Kong, which in 2002 had a 34 per cent share of the FDI market while Singapore had 4 per cent. In the scheme of investment patterns, Singapore is a minor player in the Chinese market although China is an important investment destination for Singapore. This smallness within the Chinese market is a handicap that has exacerbated Singapore's experiences in China, as seen elsewhere in this report.

The largest recipient of investments in China is Guangdong Province (see Figure 1.4). Its proximity to Hong Kong cannot be ignored. Hong

FIGURE 1.3
China's FDI Inflow by % Share 2002

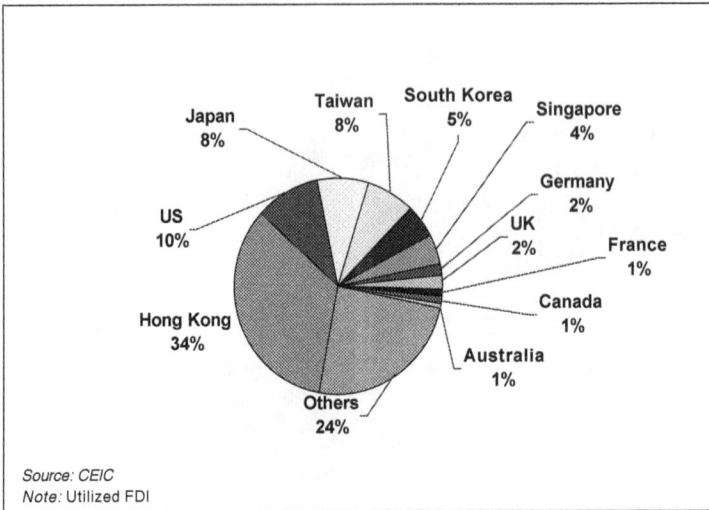

Japan
8%

Taiwan
8%

South Korea
5%

Singapore
4%

US
10%

Germany
2%

UK
2%

France
1%

Hong Kong
34%

Canada
1%

Australia
1%

Others
24%

Source: CEIC
Note: Utilized FDI

FIGURE 1.4
China's Regional Distribution of Utilized FDI 2002

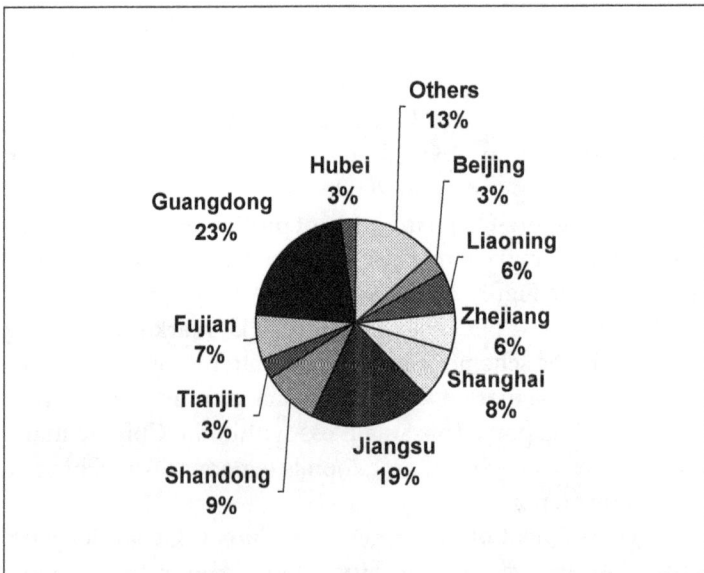

Others
13%

Hubei
3%

Beijing
3%

Guangdong
23%

Liaoning
6%

Fujian
7%

Zhejiang
6%

Tianjin
3%

Shanghai
8%

Shandong
9%

Jiangsu
19%

FIGURE 1.5
China Exports by Top Export Destinations 1993, 2002

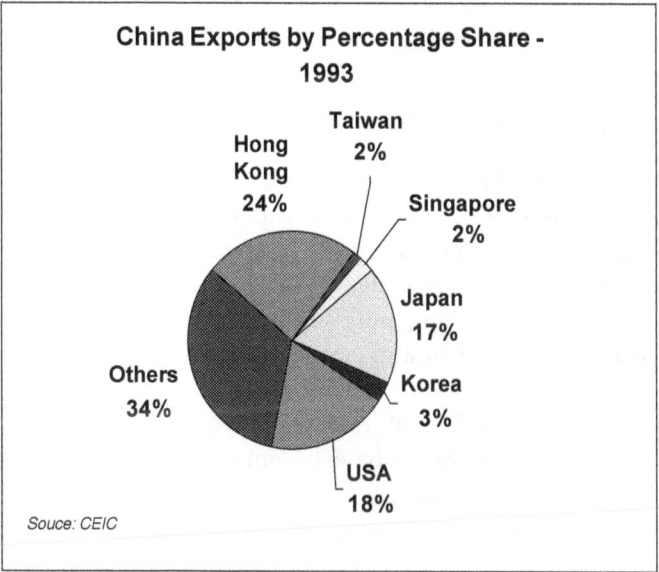

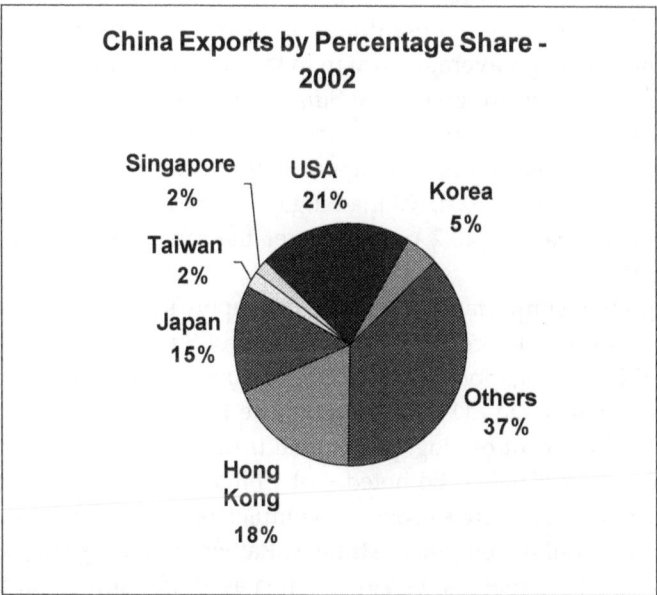

**China Exports by Percentage Share -
1993**

Taiwan
Hong   2%
Kong
24%   Singapore
                          2%

                          Japan
                          17%
Others   Korea
34%   3%

                    USA
                    18%
Souce: CEIC

**China Exports by Percentage Share -
2002**

Singapore   USA
2%   21%   Korea
                            5%
Taiwan
2%
Japan
15%
                          Others
                          37%
Hong
Kong
18%

Kong has been an important investor and promoter of Guangdong's position through direct investments and the relocation of Hong Kong's manufacturing capability into the Pearl River Delta which includes the Special Economic Zones (SEZs) of Shenzhen and Zhuhai.[8]

China-Singapore Trade Structure

While investments show one aspect of the growing economic relations between China and the rest of the world, an equally important element in this mosaic is the growing importance of trade. China has become one of Singapore's top export destinations, with exports to China reaching US$10.4 billion in 2003. It is now Singapore's fifth most important export market. China, over the years, has also become one of Asia's most important trading nations.

Singapore's share of China's exports, however, has remained at 2 per cent while the USA and Korea have become more important (see Figure 1.5). Once again, there is an asymmetry of importance. China is more important to Singapore as its trading partner than Singapore is to China as its trading partner.

China-Singapore bilateral trade grew fourfold in the last decade, from S$5.4 billion 1991 to S$22.4 billion in 2001. In 2003, the trade figure reached S$36.9 billion, representing a 31.3 per cent year-on-year increase (see Table 1.3). High average growth in the 2001–03 period with China is all the more significant given that Singapore registered negative growth with most other major trading partners over the same period.

China has, thus, become an important trade anchor for Singapore and by the end of April 2004, China-Singapore trade amounted to S$14.7 billion, an increase of 40.2 per cent over the same period year-on-year (Table 1.4).

The growing importance of China to Singapore's trade is more apparent when it is seen that it constituted 8 per cent of Singapore's total trade in 2003, making it Singapore's fifth largest trading partner, behind Malaysia, the United States, the EU and Japan (Figure 1.6). Ten years earlier, it was just under 3 per cent of Singapore's total trade.

In summary it has to be noted that China has become an important component of Singapore's economic complexion and is now an indelible part of its overall development strategy. Rather than just seeing China as a competitor, Singapore is engaging China as an investment and trading

FIGURE 1.6
Singapore's Top Trading Partners 2003

Singapore's Top Trading Partners 2003 (% Share)

Others 18%
Philippines 2%
Australia 2%
South Korea 4%
Thailand 4%
Taiwan 5%
Hong Kong 6%
China 8%
Japan 9%
EU 13%
United States 13%
Malaysia 16%

Source: Dept. of Statistics Singapore

TABLE 1.3
Annual China-Singapore Bilateral Trade

Trade	2001		2002		2003	
	(S$ bn)	YOY % growth	(S$ bn)	YOY % growth	(S$ bn)	YOY % growth
Total trade	22.4	4.1	28.1	25.3	36.9	31.3
Imports	12.9	5.1	15.9	22.9	19.3	21.6
Exports	9.5	2.8	12.3	28.5	17.6	43.8
Domestic Exports	5.3	–	7.1	34.2	10.0	41.1
Re-exports	4.3	6.2	5.1	21.5	7.6	47.4

Source: IE Singapore

partner for long-term, sustainable growth. For Singapore, China is both an important investment destination as well as a core trading partner. For China, however, Singapore is a more minor partner in its longer-term game plan given that Hong Kong, Taiwan, Japan and Korea play a more

TABLE 1.4
China-Singapore Trade Performance, January–April 2004

Trade	S$ thousand	% growth y-o-y
Total Trade	14,745,006	40.2
Imports from China	7,260,443	30.9
Exports to China	7,484,564	50.6
Domestic Exports	4,199,848	41.5
Re-exports	3,284,715	64.0

Source: IE Singapore

prominent role in its economic infrastructure. This asymmetry of relative importance as perceived by the two countries also shadows their respective views about each other.

SINGAPORE IN LIAONING AND ZHEJIANG

One way of redressing this asymmetry of interests is to widen investment and trade linkages so that Singapore carves out a niche and becomes a more significant component of China's economic progress. Singapore has, therefore, been actively seeking investment opportunities in provinces that have become more prominent in recent years. It has been building a network of provincial and city government, and private business, relations in these other provinces.

In the initial years of China's open-door policy the focus was on the Special Economic Zones, which was subsequently followed by further opening of the coastal provinces. Guangzhou, Fujian and Shanghai became important destinations for investors in this expansion of China's open-door policy. Other provinces soon followed suit, but they were less successful than these earlier ones. Now that the early provinces have become more competitive with rising operating costs and a consolidation of returns to investment, the second tier provinces have become attractive investment partners. Liaoning and Zhejiang, both coastal provinces, have been latecomers to this process but have become the new locations of

FIGURE 1.7
Map of China

choice for investors. Singapore agencies have been active in both Liaoning and Zhejiang, seeking business opportunities and assisting Singapore businesses to find niches in the respective provinces.

Liaoning

The province of Liaoning is located in Northeast China, bordering North Korea. The capital, Shenyang, and the port city, Dalian, both enjoy preferential policies as coastal open cities. Liaoning is rich in mineral resources with substantial deposits of coal and iron ore. It is also the fourth largest producer of crude oil in China. There are also significant reserves of boron, magnesite, diamonds and jade in the province. The availability of iron ore and coal naturally makes it an important producer of steel and iron, and in the development of heavy industry in China.

FIGURE 1.8
Liaoning Province

Economy

Liaoning has a population of over 42 million with a GDP per capita of 12,900 Renminbi (2002 figures). It is one of China's most important heavy industry production bases, with heavy industrial output amounting to around Rmb 367 billion in 2001. The major heavy industries include petrochemicals, iron and steel, machinery and transport equipment, coal, metallurgy, shipbuilding, construction materials, paper manufacturing (see Table 1.5). Liaoning is China's second most important producer of steel and the third most important producer of iron. Light industries in the province include food processing, textiles and garments, chemical fibres, knitting, silk, and electronics. Light industrial output in 2001 was around Rmb 81 billion. Dalian, the main port in the province, is a major fashion centre in China, hosting the annual China Dalian International Garment Fair.

Around 10 per cent of China's large and mid-sized state-owned enterprises (SOEs) are in Liaoning, although there are a growing number of private enterprises which contribute around 45 per cent of the province's GDP. The contribution of private enterprises has grown at an average of 14 per cent between 2001 and 2003.

Liaoning's exports grew by 12.4 per cent between 2001 and 2002, with the main export markets being Japan, USA, Korea, Hong Kong and the EU. Total exports in 2001 amounted to US$12.1 billion. Total import value in 2002 was US$11.4 billion, a growth of 10.5 per cent over the previous year. The major import items included machinery, electronic equipment and components, fertilizers, raw materials and chemicals.

As shown in Table 1.6, foreign investments contribute significantly to Liaoning's trade structure. Foreign Invested Enterprises (FIEs) have consistently accounted for more than half of exports from and imports into the province. The main import sources were Japan, Korea, USA, Germany and Australia. Singapore does not figure prominently in Liaoning's imports but it is an important export destination. Singapore's exports to Liaoning amounted to around US$96 million in 2001 while imports from Liaoning were about US$519 million (Table 1.7). While these figures seem impressive, in the wider constellation of Liaoning's total trade with the rest of the world, it is small. Liaoning's trade with Singapore is about 3 per cent of its total trade while with Japan it is 37 per cent, and with Korea it is 12 per cent.

TABLE 1.5
Industrial Output Share of Leading Industry Groups, 2001

	% share of total industrial output
Petroleum and chemicals	22.9
Metal melting and pressing	15
Transport equipment production	6.9
Electronic and telecommunications	5.6
Food production	4.9

Source: Liaoning Statistical Yearbook 2002

TABLE 1.6
Liaoning Exports and Imports, 2000–02

	2000		2001		2002	
	Value (US$ bn)	% Change y-o-y	Value (US$ bn)	% Change y-o-y	Value (US$ bn)	% Change y-o-y
Exports	10.6	30.9	10.7	1.5	12.1	12.4
– by FIEs	6.3	43.2	6.3	0.9	7.2	14.3
Imports	9.5	46.2	10.3	8.6	11.4	10.5
– by FIEs	6.1	56.4	5.9	–2.4	6.3	6.3

Source. Liaoning Statistical Yearbook 2002

TABLE 1.7
Liaoning's Top Trading Partners, 1999–2001

Liaoning: Top Import Partners				Liaoning: Top Export Partners			
	1999	2000	2001		1999	2000	2001
	US$ million				US$ million		
1 Japan	2167.7	2801.9	2871.8	1 Japan	3391.0	4444.3	4529.3
2 South Korea	1015.0	1475.9	1345.0	2 USA	1041.1	1509.8	1466.0
3 USA	488.0	530.5	729.6	3 South Korea	701.3	1005.4	1073.5
4 Germany	234.7	319.5	546.1	4 Singapore	356.0	385.4	518.9
5 Australia	102.6	132.8	186.2	5 Netherlands	318.2	425.1	454.7
6 Brazil	7.7	31.6	165.4	6 Hong Kong	312.7	366.9	335.4
7 Russia	83.1	152.0	159.8	7 North Korea	138.2	221.8	283.9
8 Italy	37.6	79.4	136.7	8 Germany	260.2	260.6	258.2
9 UK	50.9	37.6	113.7	9 UK	106.0	131.5	123.2
10 North Korea	19.0	14.1	106.1	10 Malaysia	143.8	151.9	121.6
11 Canada	59.6	98.1	96.4	11 Australia	57.6	82.6	114.6
12 Singapore	73.7	69.4	96.1	12 Russia	76.1	84.8	102.3
Total Imports	5530.0	8170.0	8800.0	**Total Exports**	8200.0	10850.0	11110.0

Source. Liaoning Statistical Yearbook 2002

Liaoning has also been attracting significant amounts of foreign investment in northeast China. In 2001, the total contracted FDI was US$5.5 billion, most (51 per cent) of which was directed to manufacturing, followed by real estate (21 per cent) (see Table 1.8).

Hong Kong is the largest source of foreign investments in Liaoning with a contracted amount of US$1.5 billion in 2001 (see Table 1.9). This amount accounts for 28 per cent of the province's total contracted FDI. The other major investors are Japan, USA, Korea and Taiwan. The most popular locations for investments are the port city of Dalian and the capital, Shenyang, although there are investments being made in the cities of Anshan, Dandong and Yingkou by investors from Hong Kong. Companies such as General Electric, Siemens, Mitsubishi, Toshiba, Sanyo, Hyundai and Pohang produce televisions, video recorders, airconditioners, refrigeration equipment, automobiles and steel in Liaoning.

TABLE 1.8
Liaoning Contracted FDI Breakdown by Industry, 2000–01

Sector	2000		2001	
	No. of Investments	Amount US$10,000	No. of Investments	Amount US$10,000
Manufacturing	1299	255310	1220	282646
Real Estate	94	127864	87	113904
Farming, Forestry and Fishery	74	25526	92	38889
Services	144	38023	179	32108
Construction	35	12306	48	24084
Wholesale and Retail Trade	166	28750	181	21433
Energy, gas and water production	3	6050	6	10979
Transportation, Post and Communications	13	9748	11	6698
Others	55	14198	52	15908
Total FDI	1883	517775	1876	546649

Source. Liaoning Statistical Yearbook 2002

TABLE 1.9

Liaoning — Contracted and Utilized FDI by Top Investing Countries, 2000–01

US$10,000	2000		2001	
	Contracted	Utilized	Contracted	Utilized
Hong Kong	138766	66398	152981	101211
Japan	62177	44910	70483	65881
USA	89316	47045	121822	41460
South Korea	50789	26405	49935	26919
Taiwan	27814	7427	28435	14681
Singapore (10th largest investor)	9429	7452	10371	6575
Total	517775	255219	546649	311293

Source: Liaoning Statistical Yearbook 2002

Although Liaoning is an important heavy industry centre, it also has a sizeable consumer market with a population of over 42 million. Retail sales totalled Rmb 203.5 billion in 2001, and had grown by over 10 per cent on the previous year.

Infrastructure

Infrastructure developments have been gathering pace in the province in recent years. In the Tenth Five-Year Plan, the Liaoning government announced that it would embark on a decade of investments to compete with other industrial cities in northeastern China. These plans include port development, highways and railway improvements, and airport facilities construction.

The two important cities of Dalian and Jinzhou have been singled out for improvement of their port facilities. Dalian is the fourth largest container port in cargo handling tonnage in China. The Port of Singapore Authority (PSA) is a partner in Dalian port improvement and operations. Meanwhile, a new port in Panjin, located on the Bohai Rim, has been opened and is slated to handle commodities and oil products from the Liaohe Oilfield.

The Dalian city and the Liaoning provincial governments also intend to open a Rmb10 billion expressway to the capital, Shenyang, by 2004. The eight-lane expressway is expected to reduce driving time by half from the current four hours. It is being designed to facilitate both port-bound cargo shipments and business travel. A new passenger railway line from Dalian to Harbin is also planned and will reduce the current trip to four hours while reducing travelling time to Shenyang to two hours. Liaoning has two international airports, the Shenyang Taoxian International Airport and the Dalian Zhoushuizi International Airport, and four provincial airports in Dandong, Jinzhou, Zhaoyang and Changhai. There are plans to replace the Dalian city airport.

Zhejiang

Zhejiang is located in the Southern part of the Yangtze River Delta on the southeast coast of China. It borders, to the northeast, Shanghai, the country's largest city. Hangzhou is the provincial capital. Most of the coastal cities and towns are open to foreign investors. These include Hangzhou, Ningbo, Wenzhou, Jinhua, Yiwu, Shaoxing among others.

The Northeast, closest to Shanghai, has more developed industries than the other parts of the province. The main industrial production bases are located at Hangzhou, Ningbo, Wenzhou, Jiaxing, Huzhou, Shaoxing, Jinhua, Quzhou, Zhoushan, Taizhou and Lishui. The province's coastline is the longest in China, totaling some 6,500 km. With more than 3,000 offshore islands, the largest being Zoushan, Zhejiang is also a leading supplier of both ocean and freshwater fish and shellfish. Zhejiang is rich in non-metallic mineral reserves and its seaboard has rich reserves of petroleum and natural gas.

Economy

Zhejiang has a population of around 46.5 million with a GDP per capita of about Rmb 17,700 (2002 figures). Provincial GDP grew by over 14 per cent between 2002 and 2003 to reach Rmb 940 billion. The industrial sector contributed over 57 per cent of this GDP, increasing its share from 46 per cent in 2002.

Zhejiang is China's fourth largest industrial production base after Guangdong, Jiangsu and Shandong. The private sector plays an important role in the province's economic development, accounting for 90 per cent of the province's GDP and for over 84 per cent of the province's total industrial output. The province's industrial structure has long been dominated by

FIGURE 1.9
Zhejiang Province

TABLE 1.10
Zhejiang: Composition of GDP 1980, 2001, 2002

Sector	1980	2001	2002
Primary	36.0	10.3	8.9
Secondary	46.8	51.3	51.1
of which Industry	41.0	46.0	45.9
Tertiary	17.3	38.4	40.0

Source. Zhejiang Statistical Yearbook 2002

light industry which contributes to 62 per cent of the total industrial output. Zhejiang enjoys a competitive edge in the manufacturing sector, which includes garments, chemical fibers, leather, foodstuffs, plastics, metal products, and paper. The province produces about one-third of the country's total raw silk and brocade. Other sectors that have enjoyed strong growth include electro-mechanical light manufacturing, electronics, chemical, petrochemicals and pharmaceuticals.

Zhejiang has an impressive research and development capacity, which is among the most advanced in China. It has 237 independent and 400 university-sponsored research institutes working in areas such as silicon materials, nuclear science, computer technology, fibre optics, electronics, recycling and industrial chemicals. The United Nations has, in conjunction with the provincial government, also established research centres in rice cultivation, hydropower, and light construction materials. The province has embarked on promoting high technology industries such as information technology (IT), bio- and medical technologies, and new materials in its quest to be a leader in the science and technology sector in China. Three economic development belts have been zoned in the province to facilitate these projects.

Singapore's investments in the province have increased exponentially in recent years. In the first six months of 2004 alone, Singapore's contracted FDI in Zhejiang reached US$236 million, an increase of 83.6 per cent over

TABLE 1.11
Zhejiang: Output Share of Leading Industry Groups, 2001

	% share of total industrial output
Leading New Industries	
Electronic and telecommunications	4.2
Electric equipment and machinery	8.4
Petroleum and chemistry	11.0
Leading Traditional Industries	
Textile and garments	24.4
Food and beverage	5.3
Ordinary machinery manufacturing	6.2

Source: Zhejiang Statistical Yearbook 2002

the same period last year. As at the end of 2003 Singapore companies invested over US$700 million in Zhejiang, making Singapore the province's sixth largest foreign investor. Once again, these investments have to be seen in context. Hong Kong is the top investor in Zhejiang, with over 37 per cent of the utilized FDI in 2003. Singapore, in comparison, is a minor participant, contributing 1.4 per cent of the utilized FDI during the same year.

At the end of 2003, Zhejiang's foreign trade totalled just over US$61 billion having grown at 46 per cent from the previous year. Exports were valued at US$41.6 billion, a growth of 41.5 per cent, while imports were around US$20 billion, having expanded by 58 per cent. The major export goods were garments, textiles, shoes and other light manufactures. The main import items were commodities, fertilizers, petrochemicals, rubber, electronics, iron and steel, and machinery and equipment.

Hong Kong is Zhejiang's fourth largest export destination with US$1.9 billion being exported there in 2003. In comparison, Singapore's total trade with Zhejiang was US$854 million in 2003, having grown by over 70 per cent in 2002. In exports alone, Hong Kong has a dominant presence that is almost five times larger than that of Singapore in its trade relations with Zhejiang.

TABLE 1.12
Zhejiang: Contracted and Utilized FDI by Top Investing Countries, 2001–03

Country/	2001		2002		2003	
US$10,000	Contracted	Utilized	Contracted	Utilized	Contracted	Utilized
Hong Kong	146025	66939	230144	109672	474301	201980
Japan	37543	24827	46099	31958	58148	41120
Taiwan	72542	27696	86485	29357	91139	38689
USA	49238	25858	68871	29204	111949	42022
South Korea	23118	8858	19362	8672	28448	16503
Singapore	12267	5985	−626	6883	16644	7813
France	8663	5596	6329	5976	14198	8721
Total	501588	221162	678912	316002	1205014	544936

Source: Zhejiang Foreign Trade and Economic Cooperation Bureau (ZFTEC)

TABLE 1.13
Zhejiang: Top Exports and Imports, 2000–02

Zhejiang: Value of Top 10 Imported Goods

No	Item	2000	2001	2002
		Value in US$10,000		
1	Primary Plastics	61,790	71,158	85,014
2	Textile Machinery	37,126	50,909	86,411
3	Rolled Steel	36,623	40,563	81,271
4	Mobile Telephone (handheld/car)	24,955	22,248	53,711
5	Telephthatic Acid	8,117	18,613	51,363
6	Integrated Circuits and Micro-electric Module	14,143	28,462	39,673
7	TV/Radio Sets and Radio Communication	19,176	48,179	39,320
8	Waste Copper	22,571	39,576	34,409
9	LPG and other Hydrocarbon Gas	6,260	13,313	29,141
10	Machine Tools	9,680	14,792	18,923

Zhejiang: Value of Top 10 Exported Goods

No	Item	2000	2001	2002
		Value in US$10,000		
1	Garments	509,747	586,074	672,238
2	Textiles	221,902	286,426	409,021
3	Shoes	58,819	79,749	113,214
4	Plastic Articles	38,551	46,192	65,213
5	Lighting Installation	34,009	41,940	58,453
6	Travelling Articles	36,155	38,127	49,328
7	Furniture	24,460	31,199	45,879
8	Seawater Aquatic Products	48,289	48,545	43,645
9	Bedding	24,523	28,047	36,055
10	Pharmaceutical Products	21,433	26,600	35,737

Source: Zhejiang Foreign Trade and Economic Cooperation Bureau (ZFTEC)

TABLE 1.14
Zhejiang — Singapore Trade, 2001–03
(In US$ millions)

Items	2001	2002	% Change 2001–2002	2003	% Change 2002–2003
Imports from Zhejiang	234.9	313.4	33.4	450.5	44.0
Exports to Zhejiang	113.3	197.1	74.0	403.8	74.0
Total trade	348.2	501.5	44.0	854.3	70.3

Source: Zhejiang Foreign Trade and Economic Cooperation Bureau (ZFTEC)

Infrastructure

As elsewhere in the burgeoning Chinese economy, Zhejiang is also in the throes of infrastructure development and improvement to keep up with internal competition for investments. There are more than 50 ports along Zhejiang's coastline, with the ports of Ningbo, Wenzhou, Shenjiamen and Haimen all open to foreign vessels. Ningbo is the largest in the province, and also the second largest port in China in terms of cargo handling capacity. The inland water transport system is well developed with a dense network of rivers and canals making water transport an important and common part of daily life. In the recent Tenth Five-Year Plan, Zhejiang has committed Rmb 2.3 billion to improve this waterborne network. The port of Beilun in Ningbo, one of China's four major deep-water ports, has shipping connections to 225 ports in 57 countries worldwide. The second-phase of the expansion of Beilun Port is under construction and is aimed at making it a major outer port for Shanghai in its bid to become an international transportation centre.

Hangzhou is the province's capital and transportation hub. The Wenzhou Shuangyu Highway Transport Station should be completed by 2005 and is expected to become the main transportation centre in the province. A total investment of Rmb 13 billion has been slated for building and upgrading existing expressways. The province has 7 civilian airports, of which Hangzhou, Ningbo and Wenzhou accept international flights. China Airlines has recently launched a direct service connecting Hangzhou, the capital of east China's Zhejiang Province, with Singapore. This is the city's second international air route after the first was set up between Hangzhou and Seoul, capital of the Republic of Korea, in late 2003.

POSITIONING SINGAPORE IN LIAONING AND ZHEJIANG

As can be seen from the earlier perspectives on Liaoning and Zhejiang, both provinces are re-inventing themselves to become an integral part of the more aggressive economic revolution being championed in China. In Liaoning the need for better infrastructure to facilitate investments while diversifying away from the heavy industry base appears to be the way forward. In Zhejiang, the strategy is to move up the value added ladder to become a base for more technology intensive manufacturing. Both these thrusts fit with Singapore's overall strategy of creating an economic space for Singapore businesses in China and have been followed by a recent institutionalized effort to focus on Liaoning and Zhejiang by Singapore government agencies.

The Singapore-Liaoning Economic and Trade Council (SLETC) was set up in November 2003, with leadership from government officials of both sides. The council will serve as the main channel through which Singapore will support China's revitalization of its north-east provinces. Some of the key proposed projects are:

- Automotive park in Shenyang's Hunnan New District
- A petrochemical park in Fushan City
- Second phase of Dalian container terminal development
- A ship-building and accessories park in Dalian City
- Second phase development of the Dalian IT park
- A Suzhou-style industrial park in Yingkou city
- An inland port in Shenyang's Hunnan New District

These identified projects focus on the planning, development and management of industrial and business parks and port facilities, a move that leverages on Singapore's traditional strengths.[9] In April 2004, a trade mission organized under the auspices of the SLETC visited four Liaoning cities — Shenyang, Dalian, Fushan and Yingkou — to seek investment and trade opportunities. A formal SLETC meeting was held in Shenyang.

The Singapore-Zhejiang Economic and Trade Council (SZETC) was formally inaugurated in November 2003. An economic mission from Singapore followed in April 2004, during which Zhejiang companies were persuaded to use Singapore as a first step before leapfrogging into the international market place. To facilitate this, a Zhejiang commodities centre has been set up in Suntec City in Singapore under the auspices of the SZETC. The centre will assist Zhejiang companies in going global while promoting products from Zhejiang. At the same time, the centre will encourage and support promising Zhejiang enterprises to list on the Singapore Stock Exchange.[10]

Recent reports in the Singapore press have highlighted Singapore business projects in Liaoning and Zhejiang, which serve to illustrate how the process of actively encouraging business involvement works at the company level. International Enterprise (IE) Singapore has acted as the most visible lead-agency in spearheading Singapore's efforts. It identifies possible projects and opportunities for Singapore companies through its offices in China, and facilitates the development of consortia of Singapore companies so that small and medium-sized enterprises (SMEs) can also participate in larger projects. Typically, such projects involve one or more government-linked companies (GLCs) or corporatized government agencies.

The Shenyang Hunnan-Singapore Township project is an example of how Singapore and Chinese provincial government agencies, and private and public-sector corporations form a consortium to package a project in a sector in which Singapore has a core competency. The consortium is being led by Keppel Land (KepLand). In July 2003 KepLand signed an MOU with the Shenyang Hunnan District Government (SHDG). SHDG agreed to contribute a two sq km site in the Hunnan district of Shenyang for the development. The Singapore consortium consists of four parties:

- KLL (KepLand, a subsidiary of Keppel Corporation)
- CityOne Township Development Pte Ltd (CityOne) — an equal joint-venture between KepLand and HDBCorp International, HDB's privatized building and development unit
- G&W Group (Holdings) Limited which is a subsidiary of Singapore listed construction firm, Koh Brothers

- Dayen Environmental Limited, a Singapore home-grown environmental engineering company, specializing in waste and water treatment

Another typical model of a Singapore presence is for a Singapore subsidiary to expand its core business to China. Ascendas is a wholly-owned subsidiary of the Jurong Town Corporation (JTC), and is the developer and manager of the Singapore Science Park. Ascendas traces its business presence in China through another JTC subsidiary, JTC International, which in 1994 belonged to the Singapore consortium spearheading the development of Suzhou Industrial Park (SIP). As part of JTCi (JTC International), Ascendas pioneered ready-built facilities within the SIP. It has perfected the one-stop concept of providing industrial infrastructure with professional management services and now offers clients in China a choice of ready-built and built-to-suit business spaces in six cities in China — Shanghai, Suzhou, Beijing, Shenzhen, Hangzhou and Shenyang, with plans to open up several new locations, including Dalian.

One of the latest Singapore government agencies to follow the JTC-Ascendas model is the National Parks Board (NPB). In May 2003, the NPB set up a subsidiary, Singapore Garden City (SGC), to market its Singapore-earned track record in town planning, landscape architecture, and horticulture. Newspaper reports state that SGC landed its first contract in China as part of a Singapore consortium that won the contract to design a masterplan for a new township in Zhejiang. Two partners in the consortium are architectural firm SEP partnership and JGP Architecture. The consortium was facilitated by another Singapore government agency which has also been active in sourcing potential projects for Singapore companies, the Building and Construction Authority (BCA).[11]

Singapore firms have also been able to leverage on the fact that Singapore has long been a home for MNCs, who are themselves eagerly looking for investment opportunities in China. One interesting partnership, which has been evolving in Singapore, involves a Japanese multinational, its Singapore subsidiary, and its Japanese clients. Miyoshi Precision was incorporated in 1987 as a wholly owned subsidiary of Miyoshi Industry Co. Ltd. (MIC), a manufacturing assembler of precision metal components in Japan. In 1997 MIC offered equity participation to Singapore's local management, and in 2000 listed on the Singapore Stock Exchange (SGX).

The company subsequently announced its Regional Business Ring Strategy, which detailed expansion plans into Thailand, Malaysia, Indonesia, the Philippines and China. In 2002, the company set up operations in Wuxi, from where it plans to expand precision engineering activities in China, to service existing and potential clients such as Maxtor, HP, Flextronics, Sony, and Hitachi.[12]

In addition to township planning and manufacturing, another sector in which Singapore companies have a core competence is logistics and warehousing. Since listing in 2003, Sinwa KS Ltd has been rapidly expanding its services in China's coastal cities. Sinwa is a regional marine supply and logistics company, serving the oil industry and sea-going vessels. In China it has branches in Dalian, Guangzhou and Shanghai, and has entered into mutual co-operation agreements with appointed Sinwa supply and logistics companies in other locations. Under the agreements, the company licences the Sinwa name, and provides management, technical and consultancy services. In return Sinwa receives fixed fees and variable commissions.

A similar story is also evident in the airfreight and logistics business. Home-grown Singapore Airocean Ltd was established in 1988 to provide airfreight forwarding services. It is now an integrated cargo logistics group and the largest general sales agent (GSA) operator in Asia, representing 23 international airlines in 12 countries.[13] It has branch offices in Ningbo, Dalian and Shanghai, and has expanded in China by buying a local firm, UBI Logistics, which is expected to give Airocean a presence of 100 branches in China by 2006.[14]

There are also instances in which small Singapore companies operating in China gain sufficient reputation with Chinese business partners to be offered opportunities to expand their operations in China. Once again, Singapore government agencies have often stepped in to offer support. An example of such a venture is an SME consortium led by Singapore firm, Sanli. Newspaper reports indicate that Sanli was offered a piece of land to build an industrial park for SMEs by the Liaoning government. This offer was made on the basis of the good relationship that Sanli had developed with the Liaoning authorities since establishing a factory making leather car seats in 1995. Sanli lacked the resources to build the proposed International Venture Park on its own, and found partners through a Singapore government agency, the Building and Construction Authority (BCA). The partners included a construction and engineering company, an architectural firm, and an advertising firm.[15]

Summing Up

A key preoccupation of the 1990s was the externalization of Singapore's development model.[16] The government "codified" this in the Regionalization 2000 programme, which was launched in 1993. Two approaches were adopted. First, government investment arms and government-linked companies (GLCs) were encouraged to explore co-investment opportunities with private companies abroad. Second, GLCs were encouraged to take the lead in cashing in on their core competencies in Singapore by growing their businesses abroad. In addition, Singapore government agencies set up corporate entities to sell their accumulated expertise abroad.

The third, most recent approach, has been to also emphasize various China-into-Singapore business initiatives. For example, the China Council for the Promotion of International Trade (CCPIT) and Suntec City Development are in talks to develop a showcase for Chinese products, and distribute them from Singapore.[17] Also, prominent Chinese privately-owned enterprises (POEs) ready to venture overseas are encouraged to locate in Singapore, and eventually list on the Singapore Stock Exchange. At the end of 2003, there were 1,161 Chinese firms in Singapore. Some 48 are also listed here.[18]

Another recent initiative is the launch of the Singapore-China Business Net, which is a bilateral trade promotion website aimed at promoting information exchanges and co-operation between Chinese and Singapore businesses. The website is a joint collaboration between the CCPIT and Singapore Business Federation (SBF). The following chambers: Singapore Chinese Chamber of Commerce & Industry (SCCCI), Singapore Indian Chamber of Commerce and Industry (SICCI), Singapore Manufacturers' Federation (SMa), Singapore International Chamber of Commerce (SICC) and Association of Small and Medium Enterprises (ASME) are also supporting the Singapore-China Business Net.[19]

The Suzhou Industrial Park (SIP), about which much has been written,[20] and which recently celebrated its 10th anniversary, remains the most well-known of the pioneering efforts of the early 1990s. In a speech at the 10th anniversary celebration of the SIP, the then Singapore Senior Minister, Lee Kuan Yew, elaborated four reasons as to why he considers the SIP a success:

- Successful "software transfer"
- A high standard of urban planning and management

- Confidence of multinational tenants
- Financial success of the park's developer, the China-Singapore SIP Development Company Ltd (CSSD)

These four elements, can, in effect, be taken as the essence of the Singapore brand. Many of the initiatives in recent years have taken the SIP as the standard organizational model. The emphasis on the construction and management of various types of industrial and business parks, as well as planned housing estates, form a core part of Singapore's externalization drive, and this is also highly visible in Liaoning and Zhejiang.

These efforts at strengthening Singapore-China business relationships must be seen through the perspective of the broader canvas of Singapore's overall positioning in China. As the major investment locations such as Shanghai, Jiangsu and Guangdong have become intensively competitive, Singapore is now seeking provinces that offer better prospects for longer-term economic anchorage. Liaoning is undergoing economic restructuring as it diversifies away from its traditional heavy industry base, while Zhejiang is focusing on becoming an important light but high technology manufacturing location. Both these developments are within the core competencies of Singapore which has a history of successful infrastructure development and management in Singapore as well as in other locations, and a more recent strategy of expanding the high technology base.

The challenge in this strategy has therefore been to try and embed the "Singapore model" of development in parts of China where the social, cultural and economic environment has been evolving at a rapid pace. This process raises several issues that impinge on cultural sensitivities, social relationships, business structures and on the acceptance of Western ideals from a fellow Asian country. It also raises concerns over how much adaptation is needed for the transference of "Westernized business values" to China, and how much the host society is willing to absorb these values when they are being delivered by a Westernized Asian society as compared to a Western society. The following chapters offer some clues on how Singapore and its business ethic is being channelled into China, and how far China is prepared to accept what is being transferred. The lessons being learnt are sometimes contentious, but all the more revealing of the latent differences underlying the "perceived" similarities between the host and guest communities.

2

What Business People Say

Introduction

Singapore-China business relations can be viewed through various lenses. Macro-statistics tell one story. They highlight two trends. First, (the obvious) that Singapore's trade and investment with China is increasing at a rapid rate, and looks set to continue to increase. Second, as is natural when one compares a country with a population of 1.3 billion, with a country with a population of 4 million, there is a fundamental and permanent asymmetry in the relationship. China matters more to Singapore in terms of trade and investment, than Singapore does to China.

Consistently amongst the top investors and trade partners, Singapore is a relatively significant player in China's current economic expansion. There are no available statistics on the exact numbers of Singapore business persons in China, and even if there were, the norm for many is to become commuter executives, spending up to three weeks per month in China, and the remainder in Singapore. It would be difficult, therefore, to count commuter versus resident executives. One guesstimate recently cited in an article in the Singapore *Straits Times* demonstrates how relatively few

Singapore business people there probably are in China. The paper reports that "In Shanghai there are 300,000 Taiwanese against 3,000 Singaporeans. In Suzhou there are 200 Singaporeans against 20,000 Taiwanese".[21]

But there is an equally important observation to be made about relative size. The same article points out that Taiwan's population at 23 million is just 6 times that of Singapore. This suggests that Taiwan's interest in China is much more all-embracing than Singapore. This reflects the fact that Taiwan's economy is more linked to that of China. In fact, Singapore's investment and trade diversification policies strive for a balanced basket of locations, including the USA, Europe, Japan, and developing regions. Thus not only are there relatively few Singapore businessmen residing in China, but because they are generally fluent in English, well-financed, and familiar with international business standards, they are stretched across the world.

In the last section of Chapter 1, we focused on two provinces — Liaoning and Zhejiang — in which Singapore agencies have expressed a particular interest because of certain inherent synergies with Singapore. As the interest in these provinces is relatively new, we decided to include company interviews in Shanghai and Suzhou, the business epicentre of Singapore's investment and trade expansion into China. Suzhou Industrial Park (SIP), which recently celebrated ten years of operation, has come to symbolize the application of "the Singapore model" in China. We have highlighted several Singapore companies that have recently been in the news because of their China business interests. In Chapter 2 we shift focus from the macro-economic and company levels, to the people who are directly involved in the development and operation of Singapore-China business enterprises and investments.

We interviewed a total of 88 individuals in China and Singapore of which 48 were Chinese nationals (including 3 from Taiwan), 38 were Singaporeans, and the remaining 2 were Chinese Malaysians (for details, see Appendix 1). The purpose of these interviews was to understand Mainland Chinese views on Singapore businesses operating in China, and Singapore views on doing business in China. Interviews were conducted either in Mandarin or in English, and the working language of analysis is English. There was no formal questionnaire, and no attempt was made to quantify interviewee responses, other than to note how frequently a particular observation was recorded. What gradually emerged out of analysing these interviews is a topical nexus of interrelated issues and opinions on Singapore-China business relations.

At the core of these perceptions are certain cultural assumptions, which require explanation. These cultural assumptions in turn impact on how management styles are perceived. Finally, these management styles are embedded in a larger structure of strategic business and operational issues. Our interviews in China allowed us to build a complex collective narrative of how Singapore business persons are perceived by Mainland Chinese executives who have dealt with them in China. Our interviews in Singapore have gathered Singapore businessmen's perceptions and experiences of doing business in China. Three distinct storylines have emerged out of our analysis of this collective narrative:

- Singaporeans in the constellation of foreigners
- Differences between Mainlanders and Singaporeans
- Perceptions of Singapore business in China

In the past decade China has seen the arrival of more foreign businessmen than at any time in recent history. It is critical to an understanding of how Mainland Chinese are processing this interaction in their business dealings. This is a first step to proceeding to grapple with the essential differences that the Mainland Chinese perceive between themselves and foreigners in general, and, more specifically, the Singaporeans. Finally, it is possible to understand the distinct features that the Mainland Chinese attribute to Singapore business people — what makes them not only different, but unique. Thus beyond what the numbers tell us, and various government policies attempt to foster, one needs to mark what people say. What roadmap is ultimately followed, and what destinations chosen, ultimately depend on the individuals making the journey.

SINGAPOREANS IN THE CONSTELLATION OF FOREIGNERS

"Confronted with the lack of electricity supply, Singapore managers reject establishing a good relationship with the electricity company in order to secure a priority of electricity supply, as they think it is inappropriate to do so. However, other enterprises may find a way through personal connections to get

priority from the electricity company. Singapore managers believe that the correct thing is to abide by laws. In other words, they may expect to resolve the problem through formal channels. However, it is almost impossible for such things to be done in China."[22]

At first glance, this story does not appear to be related to the issue of locating the Singaporean in the constellation of foreigners. But in the world of doing business in China, the essential success criteria appears to be how well one knows — and plays — the game. The point of the story is that, although Singapore businessmen may grasp the rules of the game, they generally insist on playing by their own rules, and this puts them at an inherent disadvantage against other players. To expand on this analogy, when one does business in any country, it is necessary to understand the "home rules". It is assumed that no one, of course, understands these rules better than the home players. Other (foreign) players, then, can be measured in terms of how well they understand and play the rules, relative to the "home team". During interviews, it was clear that the Mainland Chinese assumed that they themselves best understand how to do business in China. In terms of the logic of business success, then, it follows that foreigners who best understand and play the game are most successful.

China has been faced with a flood of foreign businessmen over the past two decades, and this was preceded by several decades of isolation. The presence of so many foreigners, Singaporeans included, has obviously required some serious readjustments in China's business environment. Based on our interviews — in both Singapore and in China — it is clear that Singapore occupies a distinct niche in China's evolving understanding of the 21st century global village. Singaporeans' position is relative to Hong Kongers, Taiwanese, the Malaysian and Indonesian Chinese, other Asians, such as the Japanese and Koreans, and non-Asian foreigners.

What emerges is a picture of relative foreignness, which centres on a comparison of various ethnic, regional, and national labels. Certainly the Mainland Chinese executives interviewed on this subject assumed that they were the central reference point on the issue of "being Chinese". Phrased differently, the distinction is about being more or less "foreign". All others were then located with reference as to how close or far they were perceived to be from the Chinese core. The general consensus — agreed by both Singaporean and Mainland Chinese interviewees — is that Singapore culture is more different from mainstream Chinese culture than the cultures of Hong Kong and Taiwan, and also Chinese in Malaysia and

Indonesia, but is closer when compared with Japan, Korea and Western countries. This perspective, which has fascinating implications for the world of business, is illustrated in Figure 2.1.

Relative Degree of Foreignness

The diagram in Figure 2.1 actually has both time and space dimensions to establishing relative foreignness. Foreigners in the outer circles, it is assumed, never were influenced by Chinese culture. For those who fall within the inner-circles, time is measured mainly in terms of how long ago the "foreigners" were detached from the body of traditional Chinese knowledge, how well they have maintained their linkages with this body of thought (particularly through fluency in Chinese languages), and finally, by the strength of other competing influences, such as Western values. The space continuum relates to the physical distance from Mainland China. This can mean the relative distance of the current homeland from Mainland China, or also the ease with which one can travel to Mainland China, as

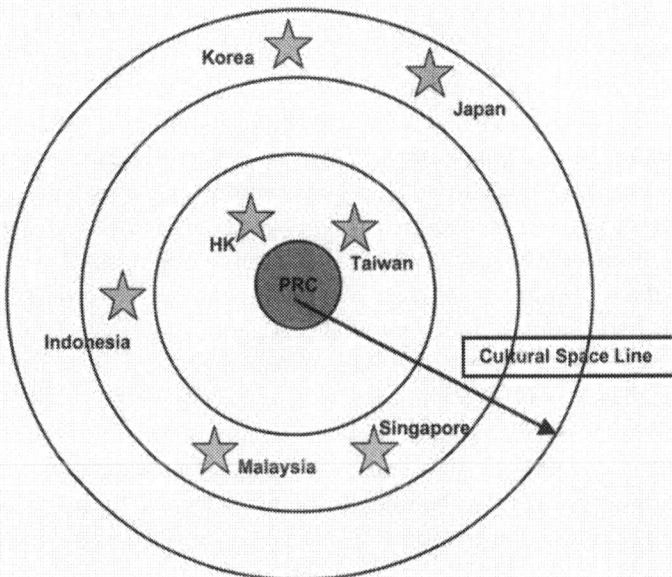

FIGURE 2.1
Measuring Foreignness

well as one's familiarity with the geography, history, and cultural heritage of Mainland China.

Time

Time is measured by the date of entry into the Chinese business arena. Several interviewees mentioned that the nature of businesses established prior to 1990, when diplomatic relations were established between China and Singapore, was distinct from businesses established subsequently. The Chinese general manager of a property management company told us that "…after 1991, many of the first-time Singapore investors coming to China were government officials rather than businessmen. They had developed a method of linking politics and business together and brought this thinking mode to China." Some interviewees saw 1997 as a watershed year, due to the financial crisis. The Chinese manager of a Singapore investment company observed that "…Singaporean investors entering into China after 1997 learned a lot from the experience of companies entering into China in the initial stage, and they also learned many things about the Chinese commercial culture from the businessmen of Hong Kong and Taiwan. Therefore, they are more adaptive to the Chinese environment than their predecessors."

The time dimension is also important because it articulates the distinction between "Chinese" and "foreign". Certainly it is obvious to all that Japanese, Koreans, and Westerners are not Chinese. Reference is often made to this obvious fact, and its impact on doing business in China. A finance manager of a Singapore company in Suzhou Industrial Park holds the view that his company is "…full of friendliness. I once worked in US and Euro companies, and in this Singaporean company, I feel we are all Chinese people. We have many things in common. For instance, we Chinese people like to communicate face-to-face. You can see our offices here are open, and you can talk to the general manager at any time. While in US and Euro companies, people are much more likely to communicate through media such as e-mail. Our company is also human-oriented and delivers moon cakes to every employee on Mid-Autumn Day."

But it is puzzling to note that many interviewees did not recognize Chinese Singaporeans as "Chinese". Being detached from the body of traditional Chinese knowledge is a rather elusive element to specifically define. A common remark was "...the Chinese don't consider Chinese Singaporeans as Chinese. They are Singaporeans." When questioned further on this elusive "Chinese identity", one Singapore businessman narrated his experience: " In the 1950s my cousin in Hong Kong bought a large jade carving that had been looted from the Imperial museum in Beijing. He paid one million Hong Kong dollars. I asked him what he would do with it. He said that he would put it in the bank vault until the time was right to give it back to China. A Singaporean would never think like that." What he alludes to is identification with the timeline of "being Chinese". This is a state of awareness, rather than a set body of knowledge.

One of the reasons that Chinese from Malaysia are considered to be "more like" Mainlanders is that they are perceived to have retained more of their Chinese language and customs. The consequence of this for business success is that when one is closer to Mainland Chinese values, one has greater rapport, and, hence, greater chances of success in business. For example, one Mainland Chinese manager explained that "Chinese from Malaysia survive better in China. They are used to dealing with difficult circumstances. In Malaysia, they are a minority. They stick together and co-operate, and they all still speak good Chinese." Their unpredictable and changeable home environment has honed their business skills. Singaporeans, on the other hand, are perceived to have lost this competitive edge due to the fact that they are nurtured by the Singapore Government, and identify themselves primarily as "Singaporean".

Interestingly, as more Mainland Chinese travel overseas, they also measure this time distance in terms of their reception abroad. Reflecting on the perceived difference in attitude towards Mainland Chinese visitors, one Singaporean CEO commented: "Hong Kongers don't look down on the Mainlanders like we Singaporeans do. They take their presence in a positive sense, and see them as clients and customers. Maybe they are seeing themselves just a few years ago, because many Hong Kongers are originally from the Mainland. But in Singapore, PRC Chinese are considered foreigners. There are negative feelings towards them."

Finally, the time element is also present in the context of the relative strength of other competing influences, such as Western values. Here Hong Kongers and Taiwanese are considered to be more like Mainland Chinese than Singaporeans and even Malaysian Chinese, who migrated from China decades ago, and were influenced by Western colonialism and now, Western values, including business values. Thus "Chineseness" does appear to be a zero-sum game. The more one acquires competing values, languages, behaviour patterns, etc., the less remains of one's "Chineseness".

Space

The space continuum relates to the physical distance from Mainland China. Thus obviously other Asians, such as Japanese and Koreans, as well as Westerners, retain their position in the diagramme as further from the physical centre — Mainland China. Furthermore, there is a correlation between the relative distance of the current homeland from Mainland China, and familiarity with the geography, history, and cultural heritage of Mainland China. It is assumed that Hong Kong and Taiwan residents are more familiar with the geography of Mainland China because of their close physical proximity.

This sense that Taiwanese and Hong Kongers are "more Chinese" is expressed as their relatively greater familiarity with their Mainland Chinese surroundings. One Mainland Chinese executive illustrated his point "…compare with Hong Kong — they do not rely on so much second-hand info like Singaporeans. They spend a lot of time on the ground. The Hong Kongers and Taiwanese, when they want to know, they fly direct to the city and spend a lot of time there and speak to other businessmen to get a feel."

Many interviewees mentioned that Taiwanese and Hong Kong businessmen are better at building up local relationships for businesses. The general impression is that Singaporeans are unwilling to do such relationship building, especially if they have to do things they don't like doing — such as after work activities, going for karaoke sessions, or spending time chatting with the Chinese businessmen. Of course here too is the constraint imposed by the fact that many Singapore businessmen are commuters, and spend their time travelling between Singapore and China. Added to this is the fact that many are responsible for marketing in a number of locations in China.

Consequences of Distance

It appears that one's position in the constellation of foreigners is fairly fixed, and it is therefore important to understand the nuances of these perceptions. It is then possible to assess the relative advantages and disadvantages of one's position in this constellation of foreigners. Finally, it is possible to understand what steps can be taken in order to either capitalize on one's strengths, or to mitigate the disadvantages of one's position. We should be able to return to our anecdote about the electricity supply and better understand what the problem is, why it has occurred, and what can be done to resolve it.

The critical question for doing business in China, then, is to ascertain what advantages accrue to being foreign, as opposed to being local. Put differently, what are the advantages of being more or less foreign? Westerners are in a category that will always be considered foreign. Taiwanese and Hong Kongers, on the other hand, are generally considered as privileged locals. Singaporeans (and Malaysian Chinese) are rather in a more fluid category. The challenge therefore appears to be to enjoy the benefits of being foreign, when it is advantageous to do so, and to be seen as more local, when benefits accrue to that status. Even language as an issue can be positive or negative. Singapore businessmen are sometimes misunderstood because of their limited vocabulary, or choosing a word with a different meaning. They have to be careful with what they say. But knowing Chinese is definitely an advantage, especially when it is a start-up company. In fact, there is little tolerance of Singapore business people who lack the ability to speak Chinese. There is much more tolerance for the mistakes of Westerners who attempt to speak Mandarin.

In general, Singaporeans' perceived foreign identity status is complex and somewhat unclear. For example, one Mainland Chinese official explained that "...due to their relatively good ability to speak Chinese, Singaporeans are not given 'special considerations' by their Chinese counterparts that are typically given to foreigners. Japanese and Koreans, on the other hand, although Asians as well, are always treated as foreigners and more frequently given 'special considerations' ". But foreignness can also be considered a liability. As one Mainland Chinese academic explained "...everything else being equal, the negative effect of cultural differences on Singapore companies in China is less significant than that on Western, Japanese, and Korean companies, but more significant than that on companies from Hong Kong and Taiwan". Negotiating distance can be a minefield in China.

Many interviewees expressed the opinion that Singapore businessmen are not as successful in dealing in the Chinese environment as some other foreigners. In order of ability, most would rate businessmen from Taiwan first, followed by those from the Hong Kong, and then the Chinese from Malaysia and Indonesia. But differently, one savvy Singapore businessman summed up the Mainland Chinese attitude "...one of my business associates in China explained why they like to work with us. He told me: 'I love to do business with Singapore because I know I can take advantage of you. With Taiwan it is only 20 per cent of the time. With Hong Kong maybe 50 per cent. But with Singapore it is 80 per cent'."

One of the major problems faced by Singapore businessmen in China is the difference between the operating environment in Singapore, and that in China. Mainland Chinese perceive that Singapore companies operate in a highly regulated, sheltered business environment at home, and hence they are unable to adapt as well as their Taiwan or Hong Kong counterparts in China. For example, business negotiations in China work differently. Most deals are struck outside of the office, or in an official capacity. One Singapore businessman likened it to a "dance of challenge". The Chinese will often start off negotiations by being extremely contrary, purportedly to test the opposing party's sincerity and temerity. Faced with an initial "no", many Singaporeans will take it at face value and back off, whereas Taiwan or Hong Kong businessmen will continue to be persistent, taking an "in-your-face" approach.

The Taiwanese are considered to be so successful because of their ability to adapt and work under the constantly changing conditions in China. The reason most often cited as to why the Taiwanese and Hong Kong people are more successful in China, if compared to Singaporeans, is that they know the situation and the commercial environment of the Mainland much better so that they are able to get closer to customers and employees. They are astute and aggressive businessmen who don't give up easily. Two traits most often mentioned are adaptability and flexibility. One Mainland executive told us that "...Hong Kong is very flexible. Everything is possible".

Given Singapore's reputation for not being as savvy and competitive in the China business world as their Hong Kong and Taiwan counterparts, Singapore business people appear to often resort to an obvious solution. They hire them. According to one Mainland Chinese manager, this boosts the success rate of the Singaporean company because "...these people are more daring, faster and more willing to take risks". Several Singaporean managers also mentioned that employing Taiwanese, in particular, "got results". We were told that larger Singaporean companies tend to employ a third party in business negotiations. As one Mainland veteran observer of the Singaporean scene related "…it is the Chinese local practice that making good relationships leads to a good deal. That is the 'homework' before opening negotiations. When they have been living in China for a longer period, Singapore businessmen can understand our customs. However, they will not do it themselves, but will get Chinese employees or a trustworthy third party to do it."

It has to be accepted that establishing these networks is a costly affair. Many smaller Singapore companies complain that the entry costs of establishing themselves in China are very high. One seasoned Singapore investor in China, who has observed the process over many years, says that "…even if they visit China for less than a week, their entertainment costs can go up to S$50K or even S$100K which is a lot money for small Singapore businesses, and sometimes, nothing comes out of this!" One Singapore general manager, who has been in China for 8 years summarizes his experience "…at the beginning, we failed in some biddings. Afterwards, we gradually understood that a key person as an intermediator is necessary. Now we employ retired government officials to be our counsellors and then use their personal relationship to seek out the key persons. We mainly depend on technology and quality to achieve business success rather than provide large amounts of commissions as what the local companies do. We never violate the law." Figuring out the best way to maintain the electricity supply will continue to be a challenge to Singapore companies doing business in China for some time to come.

DIFFERENCES BETWEEN MAINLANDERS AND SINGAPOREANS

"When a fire broke out in the workplace, the Chinese vice-general manager immediately went to the spot to be in charge of the rescue. All workers were involved as they saw it as their responsibility to save collectively-owned assets. The Singapore general manager could not understand this conduct. According to him, fighting the fire was the responsibility of the trained security department. The manager's job was to inform the insurance company. The Chinese vice-general manager and employees couldn't understand why the Singapore manager had not jumped in to join the fire fighting effort."[23]

Unbundling the meaning of this story illustrates the perceptions of the basic differences between the Singapore and the Mainland management style. First, Mainland Chinese consider Singapore businesses to be legalistic. Thus in the story, the Singapore general manager sees his role as summoning the personnel specially trained to fight fires, and recording events so that an insurance claim can be made. Second, Mainland Chinese consider the Singapore management style to be very hierarchical. Thus in the story, the Singapore general manager is perceived to follow a hierarchical structure in which each worker has a specified job to perform, and the reporting structure within the company means that each worker has to attend to his own specified job. Third, the story illustrates the fact that Singaporeans are seen as obsessively process-driven. This impression is confirmed in the story, where there are even procedures to deal with an emergency.

We can imagine that had we interviewed the Singapore general manager we would have received a mirror-image characterization of the Mainland Chinese behaviour. In fact, Singapore executives often mention three traits with reference to the Mainlanders — opportunistic, unstructured, and results-driven. So Singapore executives would have perceived the Chinese workers' reaction, untrained as they are in fire-fighting, to have been rash, and unnecessarily putting their lives in danger, and perhaps also hampering the fire-fighting experts. Also their attempt to "save the collectively-owned assets" might have been viewed as opportunistic. Certainly the behaviour of the Chinese workers, and the Chinese vice-general manager would be considered by the Singapore executives as very unstructured. By ignoring procedures, the Mainlanders results-driven behaviour might actually have made the situation worse by hampering the progress of the fire-fighters.

Contrasting Behaviour Patterns

It is acknowledged that outwardly, (Chinese) Singaporeans and Mainland Chinese are physically indistinguishable. As one Mainland Chinese manager observed "…when a Singaporean and a Chinese first meet and even after a few meetings, the Chinese might be inclined to think that there are no cultural differences between them. Because they both look Chinese and they both speak Mandarin. But when they get to know each other better, they will realize there are definite differences". Thus whereas it is quite straight-forward for Mainlanders to describe the differences between themselves and Westerners, the absence of clear physical demarcations means that an array of much more subtle cultural and behaviourial differences come into play. This analysis yields three contrasting sets of behaviour that describe the cultural dynamics of Singaporean-Mainland Chinese interaction (see Figure 2.2).

FIGURE 2.2
Describing Difference

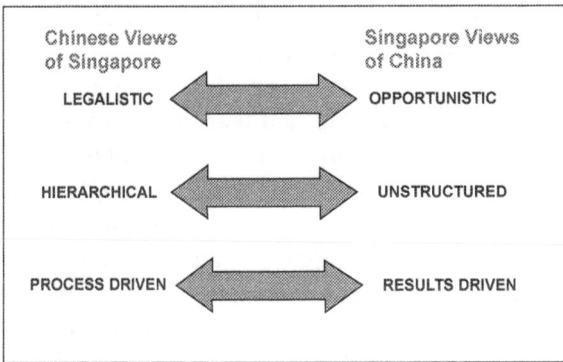

Legalistic versus Opportunistic

The hallmark of Singapore's legalism, according to several of the Mainland Chinese executives we interviewed, is the excessive attention paid to the legal document. Singapore business persons are perceived to be "steadfast" in having everything down on paper, needing that sense of security. Singapore businesses take signing an MOU very seriously, and check everything in detail. Sometimes this leads to misunderstandings as the Mainlanders may interpret this as an indication of a lack of trust and sincerity. Another middle-level Chinese manager of a joint venture explained that in their company, "...everything should be written on paper or by email. Any oral agreement will be of no effect. All communication between two sides is quite formal."

Similarly the Singapore executives view the Mainlanders' lack of attention to contractual matters as opportunistic. The Chinese are proponents of "walk a step, watch a step" (Chinese proverb *"jou yi bu kan yi bu"*) , the Mainlanders often do not lay all their cards on the table at the first instance and prefer to negotiate in an informal setting. They often do not commit themselves on paper. Some Singapore government officials expressed the view that this is a temporary situation. They view it as a manifestation of Mainlanders' business immaturity and lack of exposure to the international marketplace. They express the view that as China matures, business dealings will become less "fluid". They tend to pin their hopes on China's entrance into the global business world, "…hopefully, the WTO will change this".

Singapore businessmen are considered to be at a disadvantage because of their legalistic mentality. One Mainland executive explained that the Chinese often exclude crucial aspects of the deal, preferring to negotiate in piecemeal/ad-hoc fashion. He said that the Taiwanese are experts at closing deals this way as they protect themselves in other forms, such as progressive payments etc. Singapore business people, however, being used to relying on legal contracts, are less able to conform to this method of doing business, often insisting on an "air-tight" contract, believing it to be a legal-binding document that they can rely on in the event of problems. This is a myth, as Chinese law is still immature, and often not able to protect foreign entities' interests.

As one Chinese academic philosophized, "…it is commonly known that a coin has two sides. Adherence to rules can increase management efficiency, but over-duly adhering to rules and neglecting flexibility while executing the rules can bring about a negative effect. Rules are necessary but rigidly sticking to rules will reduce employees' morale, as they only passively obey the rules and give up initiative to work." It is achieving a balance that is difficult. One Singapore spa manager found this to her cost, when she describes the difficulties encountered with recruiting, training, and retaining massage girls in China: "…the training period is three months. Initially we subsidized the total training costs, on the basis of the signing of a one-year employment contract. The first batch of ten girls all left to work in rival spas within the first month of the contract."

One Mainland Chinese manager described this Chinese operating environment as "disorderly competition". He singled out coping with this "disorderly competition" as one of the biggest challenges in China for all Singapore companies. Abiding by the rules must therefore be considered as a weakness because "…when facing competitors who do not comply with rules and regulations, Singaporean companies are frequently surprised and confused". This "confusion" is also compounded by the fact that the rules differ from city-to-city, and province-to-province. Moreover, often the operating framework is informally understood, and never clearly spelled out. One Mainland Chinese manager illustrated these intricate nuances "...for example, in Shanghai, the intermediators usually ask for commission after they have helped you settle down; while in Beijing, intermediators ask for money first, no matter whether it can be done or not. Therefore, so far we have only sold products and never launched any big project in Beijing."

As FDI flows into China, some Singapore interviewees expressed the view that dealing with provincial officials has become even more difficult. One young Singapore executive who visits China frequently, told us that "...the provinces are very competitive now. They [government officials] have an iron rice bowl, so it is not so easy to deal with them now. Sometimes, they say one thing, do another. For example, we can have a meal today and they say this is on us, just order and the next day, we receive a bill. Same applies with policies. We just have to take it."

Some younger Singaporeans, especially government officials and those in the legal profession, are quite upbeat about the evolution of the Chinese legal system. One observed that "...generally, when Singapore companies set-up a new company or acquire assets or equity in China, it would have to be governed by Chinese law. It is true the laws in China change frequently or are amended often. But this is because China only opened its doors about two decades ago. All of its laws are new — so they are tentative and preliminary. Over time, when holes are discovered, the laws are improved. It is actually an advantage to investors."

Singapore businesses are adapting to the Chinese work environment. One enterprising young Singapore entrepreneur explains how she handles the opportunistic side of dealing in China, "...we anticipate delays and problems. Dealing with suppliers who change price or give defective goods — we, of course, don't deal with them anymore. But generally, we deal with people who are interested in having long-term relationships — we have to be discerning when choosing business partners. Too many of the Chinese suppliers are not interested in long-term relationships — they just want that deal now." Singapore business people are also becoming more sensitive to the need to participate more in the rituals of leisure in China. One Mainland manager told us that "...Singaporeans have gotten used to having dinners and karaoke parties with Chinese colleagues. The two sides will exchange views on company operations and the market situation. That is appreciated by Chinese staff."

Finally, firms face endemic labour problems, and have to find innovative solutions to chronic job-hopping. This is particularly critical because small firms are not only losing staff, but actually training the competition. Through trial and error, the spa manager mentioned above has found an acceptable solution to her problem. "So the next year we required the girls to put up a deposit of three months salary, which we paid back to them at the end of the first three months of their contract. That year we lost seven out of ten girls after the third month. So this year, we require the girls to pay a bond of the equivalent of one year's salary before starting the training, which will be refunded in monthly instalments over the course of the one-year contract."

Hierarchical versus Unstructured

Singapore companies have developed the reputation for being hierarchical, and this appears in various dimensions. In the first instance, Singaporeans are considered to be "top of the hierarchy". They generally occupy the senior management positions in companies in China, often either manager or financial supervisor. In a typical SME there may be only one or two Singapore managers in a company that employs 200 or more Chinese. The situation is exacerbated because Singapore managers fly in and out, "...I spend 10 to 12 days every month in China to supervise. I fly through Shanghai." Another perceived dimension of hierarchy is the hierarchy of the decision-making process in the firm. Many Mainlanders highlighted their impression that Singapore companies are excessively hierarchical in their organizational structures. For example, one senior Chinese manager said, "...the Singapore Government provides many regulations and requires her citizens to abide by laws. Therefore, all their work and decisions are done step by step according to regulations and procedures, usually combined with hierarchical approval, which is not suitable for the fast-moving (Mainland) Chinese market."

There is an egalitarian veneer in Chinese organizational structure that dictates that the gap between managers and workers is more flat than in a typical Singaporean firm. One Mainland vice-president of a Sino-Singapore logistics company said, "...in China, it is possible for employees at the bottom to visit the general manager's office and talk to him. The Singapore partner emphasizes "hierarchical management". The managers on each level should take the responsibility of solving the problems raised by the subordinates and no rank skipping is allowed. If an employee directly approaches the general manager, all the managers who are above this employee will be threatened. "Moreover, even if you catch the general manager, the general manager will not help you resolve the problem. You should look to your own superior."

Although it is easy to shift the blame to headquarters, a seasoned and somewhat cynical Singapore businessman with long years in China acknowledged that the impediments to success also involve the lack of initiative on the part of those who are sent to China. The answer appears to lie in the Singapore promotion system. There is little incentive for an overseas manager to take any initiative because "Why be stupid and jeopardize our careers?" A Mainland Chinese human resource manager, a keen observer of the Singaporean management mentality, observed that "...Singaporeans are cautious and conservative, even on some small matters. If they make a mistake, they pay for it". Thus it appears that the fear of failure is strong. And this is reinforced by the impression that there is also a fear of engaging someone who has failed.

This hierarchy in the firm is reinforced by the wage structure. In Singapore companies the wage difference between the Singapore manager and a Chinese factory floor worker is significant. But in Chinese companies, this "hierarchy of wages" is much flatter. In an SME employing 500 workers, for example, the Chinese manager would earn only 2 to 3 times more than the income of the average Chinese employee. Thus, for example, the annual income of the Chinese manager is around Rmb 40,000 to 90,000, and that of the Chinese general manager of a larger firm would be in the range of Rmb 60,000 to 120,000.

But the impact of hierarchy is not limited to the firm level. Singapore businessmen assume that there is a hierarchy to government organization (from central to provincial to district to city) in China that the Mainland Chinese businessmen dispute. They often cite central government/provincial rivalries as a particular minefield for business negotiations. As one Mainland Chinese official explained, "...in China one way in which the central government has handled the aspirations of the provinces is to tell them — 'You all go out'. That way, they feel as if they have the freedom to work independently in attracting business and investment to their provinces." But an experienced Singaporean CEO wryly observed: "The central government thinks they control the provinces; and provinces allow the central government to think this."

The result of all this rivalry is that various levels of government must be treated with great sensitivity, an issue that often escapes the less politically sophisticated Singaporean businessmen. One Mainland interviewee explained that "…there is a problem of tension between the city, provincial and central authorities. One of the reasons for this is that the provinces are very competitive. It can depend how influential the mayors or governors are. Usually combined meetings can be quite useless, because everyone is just polite or says nothing or just follows protocol and we need to have follow-up meetings separately. Who is best to deal with, depends on the project."

Thus relationship-building is a tedious process in China, and one can certainly not assume that because one has cultivated an individual perceived to be at the top of a particular hierarchy, that he can smoothen out the business process at all levels. Everyone must be cultivated. There is no short cut to being on the ground. This is particularly true because Chinese businesses are relatively unstructured and therefore it is impossible to simply target the "top man". Obviously also, government-to-government relations cannot be limited to the central government. Each provincial government must be cultivated and senior Singapore government officials must be prepared to travel to China, as this sends important signals of support and legitimacy.

Much of the seeming contradictions between hierarchy and egalitarianism in the Chinese system can be understood as a legacy of the socialist public ownership system. The approach to management in Chinese companies is distinct not only from the mainstream Western management approach, but also very different from Singapore companies, even when the latter are government-owned or government-linked. For example, in Chinese companies, both individual initiative and collectivism are emphasized, big gaps in salaries and compensation are avoided, and the boundaries between corporate and public institutional structures are often blurred. These traits are seldom seen in Singapore businesses operating in China. Singapore companies are perceived as very hierarchical, individual initiative is regulated, and there is a gap between what Singapore managers and Chinese workers are paid.

Process-driven versus Results-driven

One of the major characteristics of being process-driven is the tendency to compartmentalize. And we found many examples of the Singapore tendency to compartmentalize. Speaking of the Singapore management style, one Chinese manager of a Sino-Singaporean joint venture said that "...no matter what the problem is, big or small, internal or external, Singapore businessmen always insist that everything should be done step by step in accordance with the rules. It usually leads to low operating efficiency." One Singapore veteran of many business encounters in China, some successful and some not, summed up the Singaporean belief that, as long as one follows the correct process, success must be guaranteed, "...we all know that China will be important, but none of us has a success formula yet".

Compartmentalization, it is felt, also leads to a lack of initiative, and again, a fear of failure. One manager of a technology company commented that "...Singaporeans are likely to break down a process into several pieces. Everyone is only concerned with how to take his own action, according to rules and standards. They believe that a correct process can directly bring about the expected result." Of course, this makes failure difficult to digest. In the view of a Chinese manager of a Singapore subsidiary, the optimum achievement is no mistake, "...when we encounter any problems, we had better report it to the management level by level. Otherwise, no one will bear the responsibility for it." Thus hierarchy and being process-driven are two sides of the same coin.

Mainland Chinese believe that this penchant for following rules and being process-driven is a product of Singapore's stable and predictable home environment, where efficiency in process is an advantage. China's constantly changing business landscape, however, makes it exceptionally difficult for business planning, and thus there is a bias towards being results-driven. At the same time, it becomes even more important to be prepared for any change. One Singapore official suggested encouraging contingency planning as opposed to other medium- or long-term strategic plans. Given such expectations, Singapore CEOs find dealing in China can be quite frustrating. And following all the rules is no guarantee of ultimate success. One Singapore CEO narrated his own experience of watching a "foolproof" deal collapse, "...our big deal fell through even though we did all the due diligence, we had secured the supply chain, the pricing, etc.

The deal blew up because China suddenly decided to ban imports. This happened even though our partner was an SOE. What to do?"

Singapore businessmen are beginning to understand that the fast pace of business developments in China means that there is a constant race to keep ahead of the copycats. In China, business opportunism is dictated by results. A Singapore factory manager observed that at his present location he had calculated that it would take the Chinese about three years to learn enough to set up competing sites, and then he would have to move, or go out of business. In the opinion of another Singapore CEO, Singapore companies are not savvy about protecting their intellectual property in such a fluid environment, "…they are not prepared to pay at the early stages to protect IP, hence they often lose out to cheaper local producers either soon after they begin operations or sometimes, even before. This is in contrast to the Koreans, by far ahead in the IP game." A Singapore official cited the case of Korean media industry, which has successfully protected its copyright, ahead of the Japanese, who have lost large amounts to counterfeit products.

The *Guank* Gap

These perceived differences between Mainlanders and Singaporeans can be summarized through understanding references to the vital role of *guanxi* in Chinese business culture. This term defies easy translation into English, but there are endless discussions about who has it, who doesn't, and why. Mainland Chinese assume that they have it. And many believe that Singapore businessmen lack it. The question of why this is so can only be answered through an exploration of the dimensions of meanings attributed to this concept. So, what is *guanxi*? Basically, it is relationship-building, the art of networking. With regard to business, it is often associated with the Western concept of rent-seeking — primarily because gift-giving is a major element. Qualities often mentioned in the context of *guanxi* are that it is opportunistic, unstructured, and, ultimately, results-driven.

As Singapore businessmen are motivated by the opposite set of qualities — legalistic, hierarchical, and process-driven, many Chinese assume that Singapore business people are either unable, or unwilling, to understand and practise, *guanxi*. A typical comment from a Chinese manager, explaining the Singapore attitude was, "…business practices in China, like the ambiguous and non-rule abiding *guanxi*, are unacceptable to Singaporeans".

Another opined that "Singaporeans disapprove of business practices in the immature Chinese market. They consider that the *guanxi* phenomenon, ambiguity, unregulated practices and widely-existing latent rules are uncultured and unacceptable". A Singapore manager working in Suzhou summed up this dynamic, "...we are not accustomed to giving or receiving gifts. You will not be respected by your colleagues if you accept any gifts from your business partners. It is totally opposed to our values."

A Chinese manager from a Sino-Singapore joint venture in Shanghai said, "...Singaporeans are very canonical and get used to dealing in transactions by contracts. The business practices, such as commission and cash rebate, which are very common in China, are not allowed by the Singapore parent company here. At the beginning, our Singapore partner was not willing to accept our suggestions on these Chinese business practices. After being frustrated with some difficulties, they finally understood that they must do as others do in China. There exist many grey areas because of the leakages in China's policies and institutions, which they simply cannot accept."

But this is more than just an esoteric cultural matter. Chinese feel that it has a direct impact on business success. A senior Chinese manager placed a caveat on his admiration towards Singaporeans' law abiding nature, when he said that "...they obey the regulations and procedures and do everything just according to what the [Chinese] government says, such as tariffs, import quotas, etc. As a result, our company costs are much higher than those of our domestic counterparts." He continued, "...they [Singaporeans] are not good at dealing with their stakeholders, but rather are likely to resort to laws and to resolve the problems through these expensive ways". This was echoed by a Singapore executive who explained that "...we mainly depend on technology and quality to achieve business success rather than provide large amounts of commissions as the local companies do. We never violate the law."

Singapore managers thus are perceived to often lack a good understanding of the concept of *guanxi* and how it works in China. This makes it difficult for them to develop close relations with their Chinese partners. Chinese executives see this as one of the major handicaps, because Singapore companies are less efficient and suffer higher operating costs in China. They believe that the "stiff and dogmatic personality" often associated with Singapore management, obstructs them from adapting to the complex and flexible Chinese society and market environment. Chinese academics we interviewed also expressed the view that Singapore managers lack an understanding of how "informal" business rules operate. In addition, they counselled, some younger Singapore managers exhibit attitudes of superiority which makes the situation worse.

In fact, recognizing the importance of *guanxi* is often used as a gauge of how well foreigners (including Singaporeans) understand how to do business in China. The Chinese manager of a mechanical parts company told us that "...our Singapore general manager has a deep understanding of China and does two field studies on the market every year by himself, covering the northern market and the southern market. In addition, my company has specially added a course on *guanxi* to the training programme and the Singapore employees are very interested." Singapore businessmen who do understand the informal or "latent" rules of *guanxi*, must decide how to participate. Each Singapore manager makes his own assessment, "...for me, I will hire local or Taiwan people to do these things, rather than do them myself." A Mainland senior manager of a Sino-Singaporean joint venture in Hangzhou shared this assessment, "...Singaporeans can understand Chinese business practices, such as *guanxi* networking and gift-giving after staying in China for some time. However, they still think these are not right, thus they never do these themselves."

Of the companies visited in China, the majority (65 per cent) reported that they used trusted Taiwanese or local Chinese managers for managing routine daily tasks. Ten per cent mentioned that they employed Taiwanese managers only for tasks related to new business development. Fifteen per cent reported that they tended to place a premium on employing Singapore managers with international experience to focus on improving communication and team building with Chinese colleagues. Large government-linked companies, which accounted for about 10 per cent of the Singapore companies visited, expressed a preference for asking assistance from the Singapore Government in dealing with the Chinese Government.

PERCEPTIONS OF SINGAPORE BUSINESS IN CHINA

"One characteristic of Singapore company cost-control is to be liberal on expenditures of large amounts, but very strict with expenditures of small amounts. Take the choice of factory location as an example. Singapore companies are likely to choose the industrial parks with good surrounding environments and thus with

high land prices. Another example is that many senior managers from Singapore live in five-star hotels or lease villas, which is much more expensive than living in company apartments. All these factors have a major impact on the company's operational costs. On the other hand, Singapore companies require all employees to save every bit of electricity and every liter of petrol. Chinese managers would prefer to save on the big amounts and not worry about the small amounts."[24]

This observation reveals a great deal about how Singaporeans are perceived. What runs through our interviews with Mainland Chinese executives is a certain ambivalence and resentment against Singaporeans as pampered, aloof, and overly fixated on money matters. As the story reveals, there is the view that Singapore business people in China expect a certain lifestyle because of the materialistic lifestyle which they are used to at home (in Singapore). Finally, there is the impression that Singapore businessmen definitely have values that are alien to Mainland Chinese managers — although they may look Chinese, they sometimes behave more like Westerners.

The conundrum lies in taking the Singapore business model abroad. What works in Singapore doesn't necessarily work in China. In fact, what is considered an asset in Singapore is sometimes viewed as a liability in operating in the Mainland Chinese business world. A seasoned Singapore businessman working in China lamented that "...Singapore is very regimented — let loose we don't know what to do. Rules and regulations are internally created. Those of us in the field are savvy. We know what to do. The main reason for failure is inflexibility on the HQ side."

Four Pillars of Singapore Model

Four pillars of the Singapore business model emerged during our interviews. First, Singapore is known for "strong government", which is certainly seen as a key factor in Singapore's economic success story. The extensive support system is admired. But this very system works against Singapore businesses abroad, as they lack initiative, and are often viewed as complacent and too trusting. Second, financial prosperity translates into active support for Singapore businesses venturing abroad, and the ability to invest in training and technology. There is the danger, however, that Singapore firms may lose their competitive edge. Third, Singapore's stable society is so rule driven that, when venturing abroad, Singapore firms may not be able to cope with uncertainties, and understand the need to cultivate powerful networks. Finally, Singapore society is well-educated, cosmopolitan, and sophisticated. This status creates distance between Singapore businessmen and their Mainland Chinese counterparts.

Strong Government

Mainland Chinese have the impression that Singapore business people rely on the government to make major decisions for them and to take care of them. Hence they can pursue a relatively peaceful and easy life without any sense of crisis. Singaporeans are very law-abiding and the society is run on the basis of regulations. The Singapore Government has been successful in combating corruption and in instituting a social system that emphasizes the importance of obeying the rules. Moreover, this has been internalized, and is reflected in people's outlook and behaviour. There is a general feeling amongst Chinese that Singaporeans are pampered by their government. This leads to the perception that Singapore businesses are overly reliant on government agencies in terms of guidance and funding, and also a misplaced expectation that the government will be able to protect Singapore business interests in China.

FIGURE 2.3
Perceptions of Singapore

SOCIO-ECONOMIC STABILITY	STRONG GOVERNMENT
ï Enforced regulations ï Reluctance to co-operate ï Inability to cope with uncertainties ï Difficulty in networking	ï Strong support system ï Lack of initiative ï Complacency
COSMOPOLITAN IDENTITY	FINANCIAL PROSPERITY
ï Good language capabilities ï Too Western ï Lack of empathy with Chinese values	ï Deep pockets ï Investment in training, technology ï ï Too much moneyî

Thus this strong, supportive home atmosphere impacts negatively on the ability of Singapore businessmen to fend for themselves in China. A Taiwanese CEO enthused that "...no other government does as much. It's a windfall for Singaporeans. There are plenty of resources for Singaporeans and they do make use of the information. But maybe Singaporeans have become too reliant — we foreigners cannot understand why the [Singapore] government is doing so much work. They expect the government officials to do everything and they don't even do things like checking whether this industry is good in this particular location. They don't understand that Singapore Government officials are not businessmen — they won't really know where businesses do well."

Even one young Singapore entrepreneur agrees with this Mainland Chinese assessment, "...I think it is hard for Singaporeans to succeed at business here. They are just not savvy enough. They make good employees though." Singapore government agency initiatives to assist companies in China appear to confirm this view. One agency representative explained that "...the [Singapore] government is moving towards knowledge management. For instance, it tells the companies about the industry they are entering in China. How the industry is doing, who is the market leader. If they [the companies] need more research, we do have a consultancy arm. We also have incentive schemes."

Young Singapore managers came under particularly harsh criticism. Some Mainland executives reported that Singapore's young generation managers lack an entrepreneurial spirit, and seek government direction and protection when facing challenges. The perception is that they have grown up under a strong government that provided both guidance and care, and thus they are unaccustomed to dealing with crisis. They often are not adept at costing and planning and have no clear investment strategy. They are also considered to be pampered, and this is reflected by the fact that they place a high priority on leisure. To illustrate this point, a Mainland executive commented that "...they would ask about the golf course first".

Mainland executives pointed out that the Singapore Government's help can be counter-productive when businesses rely on second-hand information from government agencies and fail to conduct their own investigations and due diligence. On-the-ground intelligence is especially important in a market like China where there are many variables. Nevertheless, most of those interviewed feel that the government can provide useful support to new ventures into China as a first-point of contact. The kind of support that they can provide includes basic information, contacts with local authorities, and guidance on business processes and procedures.

Obviously the industry or sector, and the size of the company, are important variables. A majority of the interviewees concur that Singapore firms have little competitiveness in manufacturing. There are no well-known Singapore brands. Moreover, most of Singapore companies that are privately owned are rather small with limited resources. In general, Singapore manufacturing companies are relatively weak in developing core technologies that could underpin their competitiveness. So it is difficult for them to compete with other international companies, or even with some Chinese local companies. On the other hand, Singapore companies with government support do have advantages in acquiring large infrastructure and service projects.

Chinese SOEs have a close relationship with the government and thus have many privileges with respect to the supply of raw materials, the licence of land use, and market entrance approvals. For example, only SOEs are allowed to enter into some large infrastructure projects, such as large-scale container docks, and logistics and wholesale distributorships. Such privileges are scarce resources. And because of the unprecedented rapid transformation from planned to market economy, many SOEs are facing a scarcity of resources. The close relationship that the SOEs have with the government can also be regarded as a kind of corporate resource, because it can increase the company's operating efficiency and help the company block competitors.

Singapore GLCs benefit from these government-business linkages. When they enter the Chinese market through contract arrangements between the two governments and co-operate with Chinese SOEs, GLCs are regarded as partners rather than competitors. Thus they can share these scarce resources owned by Chinese SOEs. On the other hand, other foreign investors, who have not partnered with Chinese SOEs, are regarded as competitors, thus their access to resources through the market is much more expensive and some resources are even unavailable.

Financial Prosperity

Singapore is well known for its material prosperity. Many of the Mainland Chinese executives we interviewed had visited Singapore, particularly if they had been working for Singapore companies for some time. These impressions carry over into their view of Singapore business firms operating in Mainland China. On the plus side, several Mainland Chinese mentioned that Singapore businesses have deep pockets in terms of their capacity to source funds in international markets, as well as the financial support that they expect from their Singapore headquarters.

The large number of foreign multinationals operating out of Singapore reinforces the impression that Singaporeans have international exposure, and have experience in interacting with foreign executives. Singapore businessmen are considered to be very advanced in recognizing the importance of training, and investing in skills training. On the minus side, as a result of "too much money", Singapore businessmen often have problems with controlling costs. Similarly, the protected, stable environment left Singapore businessmen ill-prepared to navigate China's more complex financial arrangements.

According to Mainland Chinese executives, many Singapore companies make the mistake of applying local (Singapore) conditions when in China, hence running into difficulties from the outset. This transfer is often unconscious. Singapore firms are used to operating in a relatively small market. This means there is often an inability to grasp the scale and scope of the Chinese market. A small city in China often has a population upwards of ten million as compared to Singapore's four million. Also, many Singapore businessmen still assume China to be a homogenous market, disregarding the many regional differences. As they gain experience, however, this becomes less of a problem. As one Singapore CEO observed, "…you can say that China is one market. The whole world is also one market" — meaning that he recognizes that such a statement is too simplistic.

Chinese partners in joint ventures with Singapore companies are impressed with the state-of-the-art management systems that they bring with them from Singapore. Except for some small private companies, Singapore companies in the service and manufacturing industries are seen as having information and close contacts with the international market. They are also seen as having made investments in many countries that provided them with rich international management experience. Eighty per cent of the Chinese managers interviewed mentioned that Singapore managers are technically highly qualified, diligent, and rule-abiding.

One Chinese general manager from a container logistics company told us that "…our Singapore partners do not care about the daily operation of the joint venture very much. They pay much attention to the revenues and require the profit to be remitted to them. If the business grows constantly and the performance is enhanced, they keep silent." Another Chinese general manager from a Sino-Singaporean joint venture said that "…in fact the Singapore partner has not interfered with the daily operation. They may give you a suggestion, but what they are most concerned about is how much the company can earn at the end of a year and how much the return on investment is. During the initial stage of co-operation, I still remember we had to submit a management report to the Singapore partner every month, which even included telephone expenditures. Later the monthly-report submission was cancelled."

Mainland Chinese executives, academics, and government officials interviewed mentioned the perception that Singapore companies have abundant funding, supported by Singapore's well-developed financial market. Nearly ninety per cent of the Singapore companies visited in China reported that the Singapore partner invested in branding and intellectual property in their joint ventures, whereas the Chinese partners commonly supplied land and sometimes equipment. The impression created is that Singapore managers believe it necessary to control the company finances, often occupying the position of CEO and/or CFO. Reflecting on why Singapore businessmen encounter difficulties, one Singaporean CEO felt that, in general, Mainland Chinese had a negative, and sometimes resentful, attitude towards Singaporeans, "…in operating in JVs, they feel that Singapore always wants to have control of the money. [They think] if this is the way you want to play, OK, I'll take you for a ride."

But things are changing. The gap between conditions in Singapore and China is rapidly narrowing. Because of the sheer volume of FDI and the interest of multinationals to invest directly in China, Singapore business people are no longer perceived to be so advanced. Also now Singapore projects are perceived as being generally small size (in dollar terms), and this makes them less attractive. As one Singapore CEO quite bluntly put it, "…the Chinese are no longer interested in peanut projects". A Mainland Chinese trade official put it more diplomatically when he told us that "…now the Chinese are more experienced. Before there was an open-door policy — everyone can enter and try their luck. Now we are more discriminating. Now we are more selective. China would rather share successes than failures."

Socio-Economic Stability

With the benefit of the savings schemes and welfare system established by the government, most Singaporeans can enjoy a reasonably secure lifestyle, and hence shun practices such as bribery. Most Mainland executives contrast this with the situation in China. Such differences have affected the operational efficiency of Singapore companies in China. Singapore companies can operate well following government rules and regulations in a stable environment, but in China they have to compete with Chinese companies in an operating environment that is the opposite of Singapore — highly flexible, and opportunistic. Mainland Chinese executives cite the major difference being that Chinese companies are inclined to do what is necessary to secure business success, rules and regulations notwithstanding.

Singapore is viewed as a country that has a rule and regulation to cover every situation. Moreover, these rules are enforced. The stability of the system is derived from this rule of law, and reinforced by a comprehensive social welfare system, in which citizens receive housing, benefits, and healthcare. According to the Mainland Chinese, in such a well-ordered, stable environment, there is no incentive to co-operate, and, since the system is meritocratic, there is no need to establish life-line networks to survive. Given this safe, clean, prosperous environment, Singapore business people are ill-prepared to compete in China. As one Mainlander explained, "...Singaporean businessmen are perceived to be generally honest, with integrity. Unfortunately, these qualities are often exploited."

Some Mainlanders speculate that the reason why Singapore business people appear to underestimate the need to establish informal business networks lies, perhaps, in the fact that in the Singapore environment such networks are unnecessary. Unlike in Singapore, where business contracts are the basis of business transactions, in China there is no shortcut to spending time on the ground, which means living in China for long periods of time. Mainland executives observe that many Singaporeans are commuter businessmen, shuttling between Singapore and China, and also internally amongst several cities and provinces. Establishing these networks is a time consuming business. As one experienced Singaporean CEO told us, "...the first principle of doing business with Chinese when you first meet is not to talk about business. You must make friends first. If you don't look after the face, you can't get the business."

Thus Singaporean businessmen are found seriously lacking in EQ (emotional quotient). One Mainland Chinese official counselled that "...I don't think that Singaporeans are arrogant. But they have to learn to negotiate properly with the Chinese. Singapore businessmen may have the requisite skills or technology or credentials or clients/customers — they don't brag or show-off but they must put in extra effort to be seen as not showing off." Given that much of deal-closing takes place outside of the office, a large part of business dealings in China involve entertaining and socializing. Many Mainland Chinese interviewees felt that this is an area where Singapore businessmen lag behind others, especially those from Taiwan and Hong Kong. Singapore managers have the reputation of being "cliquish", and they are reluctant to socialize. This is deemed to be a serious disadvantage.

In their home environment, Singapore business people are perceived to be too comfortable to be innovative and entrepreneurial. The comfort-zone is buttressed by a strong legal system. Therefore, the flip side of the tendency to disregard the importance of networking, is a lack of the need to co-operate. In Singapore, there is no need for safety in numbers. But in China, where co-operation is stressed, this "independent streak" is considered a serious liability. One Singapore veteran of dealing in China observed that "...Singaporeans are like *yipan shansha* (a plate of loose sand). They see each other as competitors and don't share information." With the exception of government-initiated trade delegations, and business consortia promoted by Singapore government agencies, most Singapore firms strike out on their own. This is a disadvantage on several fronts. Local Chinese authorities are not as forthcoming in providing support to small individual enterprises with small investments (generally taken to be less than S$5 million). Also small firms have less bargaining power on all fronts. Finally, because they are less attractive than larger firms, they have difficulty in finding trustworthy local partners.

When asked to distinguish between Singapore companies and their Japanese and Korean counterparts, a common illustration is that

"...Singapore companies do not like to share information". Mainland Chinese executives attribute the superior success of Korean and Japanese SMEs in China to their much more developed information-sharing network. This gives them the advantage of stronger bargaining power as a group rather than individual entities. One Mainland executive said that Taiwanese firms have a whole value chain in the electronics industry. Japanese, Korean, and Taiwanese firms complement each other. When the upstream companies decide to enter China, they bring the downstream companies. The Japanese and Koreans thus replicate the *keiretsu* and *chaebol* systems in their business expansion in China.

The Mainlanders point out that in Singapore, the economic structure does not favour such clustering. In Singapore, firms are in direct competition with each other, rather than being complementary. Though there is an awareness of the problem, solutions remain elusive. There appears to be a lively discussion amongst Singapore businessmen and government officials on this issue. One "Singapore model" might be to designate one firm as "big brother" to take the lead, together with ten or so smaller players to bid for a project in China together. For example, in the infrastructure cluster, each company would agree to be responsible for a different area — urban planning, landscape, pipes, etc. But, according to one Singapore official, this is not happening because everyone wants to be the big brother, "...they are so competitive, they refuse to allow one company to be head of a consortium because it would seem to be an acknowledgement that that company is market leader."

Cosmopolitan Identity

Based on an overall evaluation of comments from interviewees, it appears that Singapore culture, while sharing some common roots with Mainland Chinese culture, is generally considered to be quite distinct. Singapore culture has absorbed elements of Western — British and American — culture. This realization initially caused confusion on the part of Chinese business partners because Singaporeans of Chinese descent can speak Mandarin, and have the same appearance as Mainland Chinese. But, stresses a Mainland academic, "...their values, thinking patterns, and behaviour are very different". One effect of this is that Singapore businessmen are perceived to often misunderstand Chinese culture, and in doing so exhibit a Western bias. Singapore culture is perceived to be a mix of Eastern and Western cultures. Although "Western" is often defined and discussed, attempts to define "Eastern" are more rare. One Mainland Chinese academic made the distinction between Western and Confucian values. He described Singapore culture as a mix of Western and Confucian values. And he explained that "…because of their Western education, Singaporeans appear personable and democratic on the surface, but they are actually influenced by Confucianism and admire and obey authority at heart".

Much attention is thus focused on discussions of the mix of East and West in Singapore culture. Here the issue of language is raised. In terms of language capability, all Mainland Chinese managers interviewed agree that there is no inherent language difficulty in working with Singapore managers. But the question of communication is not a feature of language alone. There is also the all important cultural dimension to such communication. Comparing the Singapore and Hong Kong attitudes, one Mainland executive cited the following example, "…where a Hong Kong senior executive might say to a janitor *"dai lo, bong ha sao le"* (*Big brother, please lend me a hand*), if he wants something done which should have been done in the first place, the Singaporean would talk down to the person."

Thus although the Mainland Chinese describe Singapore culture as "a blended East/West culture", they tend to also agree that Singaporeans are more West than East, and that Singaporeans are more at ease interacting in Western cultural environments than in Chinese. This is particularly true for young Singaporeans, who are considered to be more Western (less Chinese) than the older generation. Older Singaporeans are considered to have a better grasp of traditional Chinese culture. In fact, several older Singapore businessmen whom we interviewed concurred with this impression. One told us that "…I tell my children. Please don't speak Mandarin. Your Mandarin is an embarrassment." But several Mainland academics made the distinction between traditional Chinese culture, and modern Chinese culture as it exists in the PRC today. In the case of the latter, there is no generational difference in the general ignorance of Singaporeans.

Thus "Chineseness" does indeed appear to be a zero-sum game. The more cosmopolitan you are, the less Chinese. This applies particularly to the young generation of Singapore business people, who are perceived by many we interviewed to have a rather poor understanding of Chinese business culture, especially the "implicit" business rules in China. Pressed for a definition, one Chinese academic replied that "…the implicit business rules in China refer to business practices and norms of conduct that are understood well by Chinese businessmen, and do not need to be clarified verbally or overtly, and lie in the 'grey areas' of the legislature." Going further, the young generation, especially those with higher educational backgrounds and social status, are felt to exhibit a cultural superiority complex, which is backed up by their superior economic status.

This perceived lack of familiarity with modern Chinese culture is often expressed with reference to face. A seasoned Singapore CEO observed that "...Singapore companies focus too much on superior software and they forget about face". The flip side of not paying sufficient attention to the issue of face, is the feeling that Singapore businessmen are arrogant. This became a much publicized and hotly debated topic following a comment made by the former Chinese ambassador to Singapore, Chen Baolin in November 2003, when she told Singaporeans to drop their "air of superiority". One Mainland manager summed up the observation by agreeing that "...Chinese Singaporeans have an attitude problem. The Chinese ambassador was right, Singaporeans are arrogant".

The Western Gap

The fact that Singapore business executives are considered "more Western" is often stated. One Chinese director of technology in a Singapore software company had previously worked in Singapore for a year. In comparing the company he worked for in Singapore and the computer company in China, he said: "In Singapore the majority of the company staff are Chinese people, whose grandparents came from Guangdong or Fujian. They behave just like us. However, they are more internationalized and more open-minded due to the education in English and Western-style."

But actually unravelling what is meant by this phrase "blended East/West culture" is quite complex, particularly with reference to how it impacts on doing business in China. One aspect has to do with management style. There is "Chinese management style", which is contrasted to "Western management style". The "Singapore management style" appears to fit somewhere in between. One Mainland interviewee said that "...Singapore management would prefer dealing with dissent openly, in contrast with the more typical Chinese way of expressing dissent obliquely and subtly." This more Western approach to communicating dissent or differences of opinion is one of the most frequently mentioned difficulties for Mainland Chinese working with Singapore firms.

The use of the English language is a good example of walking this tightrope between "too much Western" and "too little Chinese". Young Singapore business people are often singled out for not speaking fluent Chinese, and for looking down on Chinese culture. One professor at Xiamen University told us that he feels that "...Chinese language education is underdeveloped in Singapore. Without the language as a vehicle, the culture cannot be preserved. After all, we can't use English to learn Confucianism and Mencianism." The Taiwanese general manager of a Singaporean company criticized the Singapore management for requiring too much English, which he felt reflected a too-Western management style, "...they require all employees to write every thing in English inside the company, even putting up a notice on the billboard. The junior managers are not able to read English words let alone speak or write English reports."

Another aspect of being "too Western" is assuming that you understand Chinese culture just because you speak some Chinese. The nuances of difference in China between various provinces is vast. As one interviewee told us, "...Singaporean think well of themselves and take it for granted that they understand Chinese culture much better than Westerners. However, they are in fact not perceptive to Chinese culture and usually mistake a piece for a whole. For example, a Singaporean may think Shanghai represents the whole country of China if he first comes to Shanghai."

One consequence of being viewed as "too Western", is that certain acquired personality traits may hamper chances of business success. One of the most often mentioned was that Singapore businessmen are "too trusting". This again links back to placing too much emphasis on the written word. One Chinese official commented that "...they [the Singaporeans] are eager to invest in China. However, they believe the written feasibility study, asset investigation, and property appraisal verification, etc., which are provided by the prospective partners. They are usually dragged into risky situations by their acquaintances." Another Mainland Chinese manager of a joint venture also told us that "...Singaporeans will easily believe something which sounds good, especially when it has a written endorsement. They seem not to make careful and independent analyses or take any preventive actions."

One Mainland Chinese acknowledged that the Singaporeans indeed had a business advantage because of their ability to interface with Westerners and their capabilities in English and Western management styles. They could act as intermediaries in the initial stage of reform and opening up in China, by bridging cultural gaps between Western companies and the Chinese. But this window of comparative advantage is closing, as the Chinese become more fluent in English, and more knowledgeable about Western business practices, and, conversely, Western companies acquire a more sophisticated understanding of doing business in China. As one Chinese manager told us, "...with longer experience and more market opening and liberalization, and with increasing numbers of Chinese students returning from abroad, this initial advantage has greatly diminished".

Summing Up

Singapore business people are in an ambivalent position. They lack a strong, distinct identity as foreigners due to their relatively good ability to speak Chinese. That is why, explained one Mainland Chinese manager, they are not given the "special considerations" by their Chinese counter-parts that are typically given to foreigners. Japanese and Koreans, although also Asians as well, are always treated as foreigners and more frequently given "special considerations" as foreigners. But when it is considered advantageous to be "more local", Singapore businessmen also fall into an ambivalent position. Singaporean culture is considered to be more distinct from mainstream Chinese culture than the cultures of Hong Kong and Taiwan, but closer when compared with the cultures of Japan, Korea and Western countries.

Small, privately-owned Singaporean companies are also believed to be relatively poor in cost-control, making it difficult for them to compete against companies from Hong Kong and Taiwan, as well as the energetic small Chinese private companies. Similarly SMEs are also relatively unsuccessful in attracting the local government's attention and support, unlike companies from Hong Kong, and Taiwan. Larger government-linked companies (GLCs) have to compete with Korean, Japanese, and Western MNCs. Here being "more foreign" would be advantageous in order to enjoy the maximum of "special considerations".

There are fundamental differences in corporate governance in China, and several of the Mainland Chinese managers we interviewed felt that the nuances of the system are seldom understood by Singapore businessmen. Mainland Chinese managers explained that in Chinese companies, the labour union and the branch of the communist party play a role, and have strong influences on management practices, corporate culture, and employees' morale. For example, favouring relatives is more widespread in Chinese companies, and in the Chinese context, nepotism refers not only to favouring personal relatives, but often political party and government departmental affiliations as well. These complexities are difficult for Singapore management to grasp or accept.

The legacy of the socialist public ownership system continues to affect the manner in which Chinese companies are managed. The approach to management in Chinese companies is distinct not only from the mainstream Western management approach, but also very different from Singaporean companies, even when the latter are government-owned or government-linked. For example, in Chinese companies, both individual initiative and collectivism are emphasized, big gaps in salaries and compensation are avoided, boundaries in corporate and institutional structure are often blurred. These differences are manifested in corporate behaviour.

One seasoned player noted that while many SMEs are looking at new opportunities in so-called second-tier provinces like Zhejiang and Liaoning, they must not forget that big players target these cities as well. Hence, it remains crucial to first identify a special niche as an advantage rather than focusing purely on lower cost-base as an advantage. The window of opportunity where this is true is extremely short. Many failures can be attributed to the business' lack of resources (staying-power in terms of finances). He reckons that one needs at least 18-month's worth of capital in order to be a serious player in China.

It is obvious from the trade and investment figures that many Singapore firms have managed to build successful businesses in China. A Singapore CEO cited the example of a Singapore textile merchant who went to China in the early 1990s looking for business opportunities. He finally located a textile factory specializing in period-costume-making. It was a business that was on the verge of closing, and he decided to try and make a go of it. He managed to break even inside of a year and since then the factory has expanded. His success can be attributed to several critical factors. Through on-the-ground investigation, he identified an opportunity that was within his core competence. And his timing was right — he correctly assessed increased demand.

3

Learning from Experience

Introduction

Singapore has now had over two decades of experience in operating in China. In the initial period up to 1990 investments were mainly through small-scale, family and ancestral networks. The lessons learnt then continue to colour the views of the smaller private sector entrepreneurs and many have learnt to operate successfully following from their initial experiences. The more aggressive investment and trade relationships have been in the last decade. In this wave there was the movement of larger investments by government-linked companies, government agencies and the bigger private sector enterprises, some of which were described in Chapter 1. Their experiences are more varied and continue to shadow business relationships.

This chapter draws on the findings of the field interviews done in China and in Singapore, and distills some of the more important lessons learnt from the Singapore presence in China. These lessons cannot be seen in isolation nor are they cast in stone. At the current time China is undergoing a transformation, and the two provinces of Liaoning and

Zhejiang provide some glimpses of how these changes affect the provincial business culture. More importantly, these changes in practices and perceptions are themselves being moulded into new contours that define relationships between the investing and host communities. In this shifting landscape it will be necessary to reconfigure and refine the lessons as new experiences emerge. Nonetheless, the lessons expanded on in this chapter provide clues as to which areas will continue to provide guidance for operating in an evolving China.

Flexibility is Key

China consists of a multitude of cultural nuances and operating environments. Each province has its own approach, anchored in local customs and behaviour, to addressing business issues. Understanding these local differences is essential to operating successfully in China. A common theme in this montage of differences is the need to be flexible and fluid in decision-making. There are no clearly defined frameworks on which Singapore businessmen can rely to engage in and cultivate business.

The operating environment in China is fluid. The crafting of memorandums of understanding, and the preparation of legal documents are only the beginnings of a business relationship. They are meant to be guidelines for further negotiation and expansion as the business relationship becomes more concrete. This open-ended structure is an alien concept for Singapore businesses for which the formal document encapsulates the business relationship in a contractual manner. In China, the document serves only as a platform for further discussions, followed by revisions and redrafting the overall game plan. This is not an unusual state of affairs in societies in which personal connections and trust play an important part in business relations.

The Western notion of a contract that specifies all the terms of the business partnership is now part of the Singapore business ethic. It specifies clearly the deliverables, timelines, nature of risk sharing and the like. This certainty in business relations allows the parties to focus on the task at hand — that of running the business and achieving the objectives that have been agreed to. This assumes a familiarity with Western norms of accounting, business practices, legal formalities and the idea of the "rule of law". China's emerging business community, in this sense, is less formalistic.

Two strands of China's history merge in a wider confluence.[25] This first, more recent, thread is the influence of a centrally planned, communist model which has enveloped the more traditional mindset that has prevailed in China in the past. The communist model does not cater to the idea of contracts based on market transactions. It is the existence of a market and the fluidity within which business is transacted that gives rise to the need for certainty through contracts. The lack of a history of operating in markets in China for the better part of fifty years of entrenched communism will take some time to be erased. In the meantime, the opening of China has meant that the Chinese are rapidly being exposed to how markets operate. There is a learning period when they become familiar with the trappings of capitalism and the accompanying business ethic. Operating satisfactorily in the capitalist mode requires the learning of Western business practices and customs which are enclosed within the four corners of the formal market place.

The second, older, thread relates to the communitarian values of Chinese society that preceded the communist period. There was, prior to the coming of communism, a traditional familial network of business relationships in most parts of China.[26] The exception was Shanghai which, with its influx of foreigners during the early half of the last century, had a history of dealing with foreign companies operating there. So is it now. Operating in Shanghai is different from operating elsewhere in China. In the rest of China and in the newly opened provinces, the emerging business community, in the absence of a culture of operating in markets, has reverted to the older communitarian ways of dealing with business. The rate at which Western business practices will be absorbed and accepted will differ depending on the depth and strength of the prevailing communitarian values prevalent in each province.

Thus, these two strands of China's history continue to colour and shape business practices. This confluence of different perspectives will shadow business relations until the dispersion of the capitalist model is more widespread and the learning process overtakes the memory of China's recent past.

The Singapore businessman, however, has a different experience of how the market operates. The more recent history of the Singapore development model has imbibed in him the need to have certainty in business relations. There is a rigid framework consisting of laws and regulations that stipulate what he is permitted to operate within the

Singapore market place. This positivist approach denies him any latitude to operate outside of the framework. There is a process that he has to adhere to, and there is the assured certainty that comes with this. This has been further re-contoured so that the operating field for him is, in some instances, more narrow as when he has to operate alongside or compete with the behemoths of government-linked companies.

This structured environment consisting of rules and regulations and a confined playing field breeds an operating culture inured to the fluidity and rapid changes that prevail in emerging markets where rules are barely being sketched. But more to the point is the creation of a culture of heavy-reliance on government initiatives and clear guidelines before being energized to participate in business. These characteristics of doing business in Singapore are well suited to the Singapore environment in which certainty is more easily ensured. They become an enormous handicap when the requisite skills to operate in emerging markets become eroded by the experience of being dependent on the public directive.

With these two diverse business cultures — an evolving Chinese business culture rooted in a different time, and a structured Singapore business ethic borrowing much from the Western world — the stage for animated differences in discourse and engagement becomes that much more obvious. One key lesson for Singapore business wishing to operate in China, therefore, is the *need for a high degree of flexibility* in operating styles so as to navigate an often opaque and changing environment.

Profits are in the Long-Term

Very quickly, most businesses realize that in China the entry costs are higher than their original estimates. This is partly due to the time needed to navigate the opacity of the Chinese business environment, and partly due to changes that are thrust upon them as the business takes shape. The lack of certainty in agreements and the less than complete faith that is posited on contracts by Chinese counterparts make it all the more difficult to define the overall investment cost upfront.

The Chinese business community is learning the Western concepts of profit, cash-flow, discount rate, net present value and the like. While many of the sophisticated operations run by multinational corporations have procedures and processes that define these financial parameters clearly, and are staffed by trained Chinese nationals, the same cannot be said of all Singapore businesses operating in China. There may, in several cases, be trained Chinese counterparts but more likely is the case where many are learning Western business practices through their employment by Singapore businesses. These counterparts have to learn and apply these concepts as they go along. It cannot be assumed that they would all understand the financial methodologies as easily as those who are formally trained in these matters. The result of this gap in knowledge is the extraction and use of poor estimates, and the difficulty of achieving agreement on cost estimates.

The gap in financial knowledge amongst Chinese employees is not lost on Singapore business. The manner in which this is being addressed by Singapore business is to insist on financial and operational control being maintained by Singapore staff. This insistence on control of the finances is seen by Chinese counterparts as a lack of trust by Singapore managers, and therefore becomes a point of contention that sometimes leads to serious financial disagreement. Chinese employees of Singapore business believe that they can circumvent the financial controls being imposed by Singapore managers. They become creative in their approach to information capture so that the Singapore financial managers obtain access to information that is only partially correct. The overall result of this lack of trust emanating from a belief in inadequate skills is that when the financials are eventually computed, the profits do not appear to be as rosy as promised at the inception of the business.

This concern with understanding the financial underpinnings of business is also apparent among the other overseas Chinese groups operating in China. They, however, appear to have reduced this knowledge gap by entrusting the Chinese counterparts more, imposing higher standards of accountability through compensation design, and employing greater vigilance in monitoring financial operations. This may reduce the likelihood of financial misreporting but more importantly increases the level of trust between the two groups. The success of these other groups such as the Hong Kong and Taiwan businesses hinges on their ready acceptance of Chinese skill levels, and a willingness to cultivate trust through greater involvement in the business enterprise.

All these efforts are time consuming and when coupled with the demands of a changing business environment in which provincial authorities, city officials, and local participants have differing priorities, the cost of operations will often increase substantially. Many of these costs may be latent and unknown to the investor until the business commitment has been made, and the initial investment has been sunk. The experience of many businesses bears witness to this unfolding canvas. While this occurrence is declining in the developed cities and provinces, it continues to exist in the provinces that have only now joined the race to become attractive investment locations. Singapore businesses seeking opportunities in these next tier provinces will therefore have to address the vagaries of a business environment in which changes will be rapid. The lesson in this expansion into the wider Chinese business environment is that *profits can only be ascertained in the long term*. Business in China offers exciting prospects, but it requires a strong stomach for risk and long staying power.

Building Relationships at All Levels is Essential

China is a complex market for business, consisting of a myriad of structures and relationships at various levels.[27] The important role of bureaucrats and that of political affiliations cannot be dismissed in attempting to fathom the operations of the market. Although the business world in China is changing, this group consisting of political personalities and bureaucrats continues to define the contours of the change. This is not unlike many other Asian countries where the political elite and the bureaucracy act in tandem to create, participate in, and redraw the four corners of the market place.[28] In China, the difference lies in the fact that the four corners are less well defined because the regulatory framework is less than rigid. This flexibility offers greater leeway for both the market participant and the referee. There is, hence, an opportunity to be capitalized on, and an uncertainty that has to be dealt with.

Without doubt, operating in the Chinese market requires an adroit hand at cultivating, managing and nurturing relationships at the political and bureaucratic levels. The referees of the market place are also the custodians of the legacy being left by a communist society that is now promoting capitalism. This should not be a surprise to Singapore businesses with a history of having to operate in other emerging markets where political patronage and business leadership coexist in mutual harmony. In the newly emerging provinces in China, the apex of this relationship structure consists of political personalities and the bureaucracy since the business structures are yet to form.[29]

In time, there is the likelihood that the emerging business elite may supplant the bureaucracy in some provinces and, in others, the political personalities. But that time may be some way off. Much groundwork needs to be done to understand these different referees of the emerging market structure so that an appropriate level of trust can be built between the investing community and the referees. It is essential to understand the role of the referee in the China context. They are not the impartial referees of the western business model. They act as trustees of the legacy being transferred by the Communist Party to its community through the operations of the market. When seen in this light, it becomes obvious that the role of party leaders and bureaucrats is to prevent the public interest from being sacrificed excessively.

As has been evident in many other countries, the role of party officials and bureaucrats in acting as both referees and participants in the market raises issues of conflict of interest. It has been no different in China. There is, embedded within this inseparability of roles, the potential for rent seeking and many cases in recent years attest to this. This is to be expected in societies in which transparency and the rule of law are new concepts. Thus for Singapore businesses in China the need to understand how far and how deep these practices run is an essential feature of business development. In this broader complexity of business navigation, China is no different from the rest of the developing world. The costs of doing business will always be higher than estimated. In the developed countries that which goes under the guise of licences, permits, and fines are often usurped by the private purses of the referees in the developing countries where transparency is less than assured.

While the need for developing working relations in the marketplace is well understood, less emphasis has often been laid on the need to break through hierarchy within business establishments. The Western corporate model with which Singapore businesses are familiar does not readily hold in China. At the factory and company levels there is a real need to interact and develop close relationships with all levels of workers and management in the Chinese enterprise. This "flat" relational structure stems from the communist ideology of all workers being equal, and the generally narrower gaps in compensation between senior and junior staff.

As the interviews have shown, Singapore managers tend to prefer operating in a hierarchical mode while Chinese staff prefer a more consensual and "flat" operating style. This is an important element in the Chinese enterprise when seen in the context of political and bureaucratic relations. Lower level Chinese employees may well be senior members of the political apparatus, and equally well placed in relation to the public bureaucracy. Alienating factory floor relationships may therefore result in a deterioration of official relations at the political and bureaucratic levels. Thus, getting the electricity supply reinstated through a relationship structure emanating from the lower level workers on the shop floor may well be the best way forward instead of depending on formal channels.

There is also the pressure of having to sustain and nurture relationships inside business enterprises by participating in the leisure activities of staff. The Chinese way of building trust is almost all encompassing. It requires a high energy level to be engaged inside and outside the office. Long dinners, entertainment and other activities are part of the Chinese worker's employment penumbra. These external indices compensate for their low salaries, and participating in this shadow shows a commitment to developing a common community within the enterprise. It is a far cry from the approach taken by most Singapore managers. In sum then, it is clear that *developing relations in China requires much energy within and outside the enterprise*. The challenge of navigating, nurturing and maintaining the relationship structure is more complex and time consuming than most assume.[30]

A Wider View of the Chinese Business World Helps

There is the often-quoted view that China is a large and attractive market. This is also a view held by most Singapore businessmen. But this is to miss the details underpinning the Chinese market. There are clear geographical differences that most business people are aware of. Similarly there are subtle cultural differences that define the different provinces and cities. And these too are often familiar to the investing community. But China is much more than this. It is a complex marketplace consisting of a variety of consumer tastes, skills, capabilities, factor endowments, technology, levels of sophistication and business practices. More importantly it is a market in transition, not just in the demand for goods and services but also in the skills, technology and labour being supplied.

Once it is apparent that understanding the Chinese business world is a complicated and, often, challenging task, the process of navigating and positioning oneself in this changing environment becomes more effective. The political underpinnings of business enterprises and their importance in ensuring anchorage in the appropriate sectors and locations are well understood. But equally important is the nature of the relationships between the political apparatus, the bureaucracy and the workers in the enterprise. These relationships are often subtle but critical to the successful operations of the business.

These relationship structures also differ according to the location. In the provinces and cities that have been open to foreign investment for a longer time, these relationships have become more diffuse and less important. In the newly attractive second tier provinces these relationships continue to have a strong influence and must be cultivated with dexterity. It is in this context that the need to co-opt other Chinese such as those from Hong Kong, Taiwan, Malaysia, and Indonesia, become apparent. They have a longer and deeper history of participating in Mainland China's capitalist experiment and their adaptability in these matters cannot be ignored.[31]

A market in which the supply-side and the demand patterns are both in transition offers significant opportunities and raises several hurdles. Increasing levels of urbanization and growth in income percolate through to growth in demand for a variety of goods and services. Appropriate pricing strategies to capture these market segments in the different locations are obvious. But less apparent is that the dynamism of the demand structure would call for better operating philosophies as new entrants enter the market to expropriate existing brands and positions that have been created.

In China, the protection of intellectual property, especially by the small investor, is less than satisfactory. This gap in the ability to protect ideas and design means that hard won positions are lost quickly as the copycats occupy the shelf-space. Accepting this inevitability upfront, and crafting fallback positions even before embarking on business ventures in China can help ameliorate these possibilities. But there is no substitute to being highly flexible in the Chinese market. The returns to investment in niche sectors offer high returns, if successfully positioned.

High returns also attract new entrants, forcing businesses to seek new ventures just as swiftly as when the competition become intensive. So the willingness to move rapidly from making noodles to participating in small power plants is an essential ingredient of doing business in a changing China. The spectrum of business ventures in which an investor is willing to take risks can be fairly wide. Once the initial relationships are built, the Chinese market offers the savvy investor a variety of opportunities. The risk profiles differ in each business but the returns may be sufficient to evoke an interest. Almost inevitably this implies a need to be there for the longer-term and a commitment to have deeper pockets than initially envisaged.

At another level it would be advisable to understand how and why other overseas Chinese communities have chosen to operate in some sectors or in specific locations.[32] These add clues to how the political, bureaucratic and business principles are intertwined in the different locations or in the specific industries. It also shows that operating in those environments requires adaptable capabilities not readily seen amongst Singapore managers. The Chinese business environment is not often transparent as many participants are already aware. Reading the "tea leaves" through observation of the successful participants, doing sufficient ground work, and becoming familiar with the local environment are essential ingredients for positioning in the Chinese marketplace. The experiences of operating in other countries may provide some value but they are insufficient for the Chinese market. There is, without doubt, a need to *have a broader view of how business operates in China* to be able to take advantage of the business opportunities present there. Due diligence and local knowledge are key ingredients for investing and participating in a dynamic market such as China.

Business Principles Alone will not Ensure Success

The Singapore approach to doing business is framed within the Western corporate model and tailored to operate in a rule-driven environment. China is different. The rules of business engagement are only now being crafted, and they continue to be redrawn as the learning improves. In many businesses corporate culture as understood elsewhere is only evolving in Chinese enterprises, particularly those in the second tier provinces. In this rapidly shifting environment there cannot be fixed ideas of how business should operate. A high degree of improvization, cultural attenuation, and operating flexibility is called for.

Formal business methodologies and adherence to corporate accountability are key ingredients for positioning in markets with a history of such practices. In China the notions of corporate accountability, intellectual property rights, accounting principles, and the sanctity of contracts are new concepts. Expecting Chinese partners to perceive business through these lenses is therefore a recipe for creating unbridgeable gaps in the short-term. Communal responsibility for the assets of an enterprise is still commonplace. In this cultural context, Singapore businesses would do well to see whether there is merit in operating with less hierarchy and with more of a collective sense of identity at the firm level. In the second tier provinces there will be a greater sense of communal identity with enterprises because of the stronger influence of the political and bureaucratic values inherent in those provincial societies.

There is also the misplaced belief that China is a low wage, low value added manufacturing location. This belief has to be turned on its head. China is home to a wide spectrum of technological capabilities. At the higher end of the spectrum Chinese enterprises are technology and skills intensive, and they have fairly sophisticated management skills. But these are the large-scale investments in which the average Singapore investor does not have the financial weight to participate. Attempting to seek partners in these ventures is therefore a more difficult task even if Singapore businesses have the technical capabilities. Seeking partnerships in these large investment businesses calls for a high level of due diligence and acculturation to the practices that these businesses have created.

The lessons that the larger Singapore businesses have learnt in handling these more sophisticated Chinese ventures is that the sums involved are substantial and that there has to be rapid response to opportunities being tabled. The Singapore approach to seek head office approval and for detailed business planning sits uncomfortably with the expectations of Chinese business officials. The corporate culture prevailing in Singapore businesses hinders managers in the field from taking advantage of opportunities being presented to them. There is also the constant fear of failure and the repercussions that this has on individual career paths. Operating effectively in the larger Chinese corporate world requires a more flexible and delegated responsibility structure that allows Singapore managers to deal with exigencies as they arise. It calls for more than just applying business principles; it requires a higher appetite for risk and more risk-taking individuals.

Perhaps the more apparent lesson that Singapore businesses learn in their ventures in China is that there is a high sense of fluidity in operating there. Decisions are never totally binding. Legal documents have an inherent flexibility to interpretation and carry less determinacy. There is an imprecision with which financial matters are addressed. There are non-business driven costs that impinge upon and are material to the business in question. There is a need to cultivate and foster relationships at different levels. All these considerations in operating in China require an open mind, and a willingness to bend the rules or to operate unconventionally. Not all Singapore businesses have the stomach or the capability to navigate these hurdles. Those that do, almost inevitably have had a long exposure to the Chinese market. In short, *business principles alone are inadequate for success* in operating in the Chinese market. There are much wider concerns that impinge on cultural sensitivities, political and bureaucratic relationships, and an overwhelming requirement to participate in activities beyond the business venture.

Summing Up

In summary, it has become apparent to most Singapore business people venturing into China that five key lessons have to be learnt. These are all related to the transiting business environment in China and they call for rethinking the Singapore business model as applied to different conditions.

These lessons can be summarized as follows:

1. To be flexible in all business dealings as the Chinese perspective is one of allowing for changes as the business venture evolves.
2. To understand that profits can only be assured in the longer-term since almost inevitably costs will escalate beyond what are estimated in the plans.
3. There is a need to develop relationships at all levels, including those external to the business, since there is a wider nexus of relationships that underpin business ventures.
4. Operating in China requires a wider view of the business world, taking into account political and bureaucratic structures, the possibility of unseen competition, and the likelihood of intellectual property expropriation.
5. Business principles alone cannot guarantee success because there must be an inherent willingness to take risks, with managers having high risk appetites, and a flexible corporate structure that allows managers to act on their initiatives without being penalized.

Notes

1   See Zweng (2002).
2   CEIC (statistical database).
3   See Tan and Yeung (2000).
4   See Yeung (2003*b*).
5   See Lu and Zhu (1995), and Regnier (1993).
6   Embassy of the PRC, Singapore.
7   Department of Statistics, and IE Singapore.
8   See Chiu and Ho (1997).
9   *Straits Times*, 8 May 2004.
10   *Straits Times*, 23 April 2004.
11   *Straits Times*, 31 December 2003.
12   *The Edge*, Singapore, 12 May 2003; *Straits Times*, 25 March 2002; <www.miyoshi.biz>.
13   <www.airocean.com.sg>.
14   *Straits Times*, 3 January 2004.
15   <www.sanli.com>; *Straits Times*, 16 January 2004.
16   See Yeung (2003*a*).
17   NetworkChina (July 2004), International Enterprise Singapore.
18   Mr Raymond Lim, Minister of State for Trade & Industry and Foreign Affairs, at the 2nd Singapore Zhejiang Economic and Trade Council Meeting on 5 April 2004 at Zhejiang International Hotel, Singapore Government website.
19   Singapore Chinese Chamber of Commerce and Industry (SCCCI) Press Release.
20   See Pereira (2003).
21   *Straits Times*, 5 January 2004.
22   Interview with Mainland Chinese vice-president of a metal works company.
23   Mainland Chinese executive of a Singapore company.
24   Mainland Chinese academic.
25   See Wang (2002).
26   See Yao (2004).
27   See Chan (2000).

28   See Menkhoff and Gerke (2004).
29   See Pearson (1997).
30   See Tong and Yong (1998), and Lio and Chen (1997).
31   See Gomez and Hsiao (2001), Jomo and Folk (2003) Suryadinata (1995), and Wang (1999).
32   See Hsing (2003).

Bibliography

CHAN, K.B., ed. *Chinese Business Networks — State, Economy and Culture*. Singapore: Prentice-Hall, 2000.

CHIU, Stephen W.K., HO, Kong Chong and LUI, Tai-Lok. *City-States in the Global Economy: Industrial Restructuring in Hong Kong and Singapore*. Boulder, CO: Westview, 1997.

GOMEZ, Edmund Terence and HSIAO, Hsin-Huang Michael, eds. *Chinese Business in South-East Asia: Contesting Cultural Explanations, Researching Entrepreneurship*. Surrey: Curzon, 2001.

HSING, You-tien. "Ethnic identity and business solidarity: Chinese capitalism revisited". In *The Chinese Diaspora: Space, Place, Mobility and Identity*, edited by Laurence J.C. Ma and Carolyn Cartier. Boulder, CO: Rowman and Littlefield Publishers, 2003.

JOMO, K.S. and Brian C. FOLK, eds. *Ethnic Business: Chinese Capitalism in Southeast Asia*. London: Routledge Curzon, 2003.

LIO, Yadong and CHEN, Min. "Does *guanxi* influence firm performance?" *Asia Pacific Journal of Management* 14, no. 1 (1997).

LU, Ding and ZHU, Gangti. "Singapore direct investment in China: features and implications". *ASEAN Economic Bulletin* 120, no. 1 (1995).

MENKHOFF, Thomas, and Solvay GERKE, eds. *Chinese Entrepreneurship and Asian Business Networks*. London: RoutledgeCurzon, 2004.

PEARSON, Margaret M. *China's New Business Elite: The Political Consequences of Economic Reform*. Berkeley, CA: University of California Press, 1997.

PEREIRA, Alexius A. *State Collaboration and Development: Strategies in China. The Case of the China-Singapore Suzhou Industrial Park*. London: RoutledgeCurzon, 2003.

REGNIER, Philippe. "Spreading Singapore's wings worldwide: a review of traditional and new investment strategies". *Pacific Review* 6, no. 4 (1993).

SURYADINATA, Leo, ed. *Southeast Asian Chinese and China: The Politico-Economic Dimension*, Singapore: Times Academic Press, 1995.

TONG Chee Kiong and YONG Pit Kee. "*Guanxi* Bases, *Xinyong* and Chinese Business Networks". *British Journal of Sociology* 49, no. 1 (1998).

TAN Chia-Zhi, and YEUNG, Henry Wai-chung. "The Regionalization of Chinese Business Networks: A Study of Singaporean Firms in Hainan, China". *Professional Geographer* 52, no. 3 (2000).

WANG Gungwu. *China and Southeast Asia: Myths, Threats and Culture*. Occasional Paper No. 13, East Asian Institute, National University of Singapore, Singapore: World Scientific and Singapore University Press, 1999.

WANG Gungwu. "The Emergence of China". Radio Australia Asia Pacific Lecture, Melbourne, Australia downloaded from <www.asialink.unimelb.edu.au/cpp/transcripts/gungwu200209.html>, 2002.

YAO Souchou. "*Guanxi*: Sentiment, performance and the trading of words". In MENKHOFF and GERKE, 2004.

YEUNG, Wai-Chung Henry. "Managing Economic (Insecurity) in the Global Economy: Institutional Capacity and Singapore's Development State". Paper presented at the Conference on Globalization and Economic Security in East Asia: Governance and Institutions, Institute of Defence and Strategic Studies, Nanyang Technological University, Singapore, 11–12 September 2003, 2003*a*.

YEUNG, Henry Wai-Chung. "Strategic Governance and Economic Diplomacy in China: The Political Economy of Government-linked Companies from Singapore". Paper presented at the Conference on Regional Governance: Greater China in the 21st Century, 24–25 October 1993, Centre of Contemporary Chinese Studies, University of Durham, UK, 2003*b*.

ZWENG, David. *Internationalizing China: Domestic Interests and Global Linkages*. Ithaca, NY: Cornell University Press, 2002.

APPENDIX 1

THE INTERVIEW SELECTION PROCESS

In order to locate potential interviewees, we first had to estimate how many Singapore companies are domiciled in these three locations. In April 2004 we found 512 in the Shanghai area (including 234 in Shanghai and 278 companies in Suzhou); 269 companies in Zhejiang; and 295 companies in Liaoning making it a total of 1076 companies in the three locations. This preliminary company list was drawn from various sources, including the Singapore General Consulate in Shanghai, the China State Administration for Industry and Commerce, and information from local governments, based on annual auditing records.

We then narrowed the number of companies. With regard to Shanghai and Suzhou, as the concentration of Singapore companies is quite high, we decided to focus only on larger companies, those with a registered capital of more than US$5 million. There were 80 companies in this category. In Zhejiang and Liaoning we limited our samples to three cities. In Zhejiang we found 125 companies in Hangzhou and Ningbo, and in Liaoning, we found 59 companies in Dalian.

In attempting to contact companies to verify their presence, and arrange interviews, the team encountered various problems — incorrect information, addresses and contact numbers, names which differed from those actually registered, and many simply uncontactable. After much detective work, initial contacts were established with 60 companies in the Shanghai area, 27 in Zhejiang, and 16 in Liaoning.

Of those successfully contacted, 67 companies refused to be interviewed for a variety of reasons, from outright refusal, to lack of time, to lack of appropriate individual to be interviewed. The team finally succeeded in arranging and conducting interviews with 40 executives, in 36 China-based Singapore companies: 17 in Shanghai (and Suzhou), 12 in Zhejiang, and 7 in Liaoning. These interviews were supplemented by interviews with 7 government officials (provincial and city levels), and 7 Chinese academics and professionals. In total, 54 interviews were conducted in Mandarin, at the companies in China. While majority of those interviewed were PRC nationals, some Singaporean executives residing in China were also amongst those interviewed.

A similar set of interviews was conducted in Singapore. These included 23 executives with business experience in China; 6 government officials, and 5 academics and professionals. Most Singaporean executives who were contacted had traveled widely in China, and it was therefore decided not to attempt to interview only executives who had exclusive interests in Liaoning or Zhejiang. In total, 34 interviews were conducted in Singapore, and the majority of those interviewed in Singapore were Chinese Singaporeans.

Details of Interviews

1. **Nationality of Interviewees**

   A total of 88 interviews were held during the research. In China the team interviewed 54 individuals of whom 45 were PRC nationals, 8 were Singaporeans and 1 was Malaysian. In Singapore the team interviewed a total of 34 individuals of whom 3 were PRC nationals, 30 were Singaporeans and 1 was Malaysian.

2. **Professional Breakdown**

   Most of the interviewees were business executives (71.5 per cent). In China, the interviewees included 40 business executives, 7 government officials and 7 academics. In Singapore the interviewees were 23 business executives, 6 government officials and 5 academics.

3. **Industry Coverage**

   The largest coverage of interviews was in manufacturing (42 per cent), followed by real estate (22 per cent), IT/consulting/education (20 per cent) and the remainder in shipping, logistics and trading.

   In China the team interviewed 24 manufacturing establishments, 4 real estate/leisure companies, 3 shipping and logistics companies, 4 IT/consulting companies and 1 trading company.

   In Singapore the interviews were held with 1 manufacturing establishment, 9 real estate/leisure companies, 4 shipping and logistics companies, 8 IT/consulting/education companies and 1 trading company.

4. **Ownership**

The largest component of companies interviewed was privately owned (69 per cent), followed by (GLC) government-linked companies (22 per cent), with the remainder amongst the subsidiaries of multinational corporations.

In China the interviewed companies included 25 privately owned Singapore joint-ventures, 8 GLC businesses and 3 subsidiaries of multinationals.

In Singapore the interviewed list consisted of 16 private companies, 5 GLCs and 2 subsidiaries of multinationals.

5. **Time of Entry into China**

Most (58 per cent) of the companies had entered China between 1993 and 1998, while around an equal number had entered China before 1993, and after 1998.

In the interviewed list in China 25 companies arrived between 1993 and 1998, 5 arrived before 1993, and 6 after 1998.

In the Singapore list 9 companies went to China between 1993 and 1998, 8 went before 1993, and 6 after 1998.

APPENDIX 2

A CROSS-BORDER INVESTMENT MODEL
by
Yuwa Hedrick-Wong

Singapore's investment and business entry into China can be viewed along three dimensions — use of internal resources, the external market environment, and the organizational structure though which business has been pursued. These three dimensions allow a firm to decide how best to approach a particular market. In selecting an appropriate combination among the three dimensions, firms also posit a specific view and expectation of the environment in which it intends to operate. Likewise, these three dimensions offer the host country a view of how the investor perceives the business opportunity and allows the host country to calibrate how much of a match there is in expectations between the two parties. The existence of wide gaps in each dimension, or in some of the dimensions, highlights the issues that arise in operating in these environments.

This approach to understanding the investment decision and the gaps that arise is a "high-level" model for organizing data and information more effectively while constituting a framework for generating new insights. It draws its inspiration from the literature of industrial organization, applying it to cross-border investment. In essence, the framework consists of three dimensions:

(i) Conditions of the quality and quantity of internal resources;
(ii) Conditions relating to the market environment; and
(iii) Conditions relating to organization structure.

Taken together these three sets of conditions help determine why and how a firm would decide to invest in a particular market, forming an "investment decision triangle" as shown below.

"Conditions of the quality and quantity of internal resources" include financial resources, information capability and data, technological resources (especially proprietary and patented products), and also, real or perceived access to government authorities in both the host country and the country of origin of the investment. A business firm trying to decide if it should

FIGURE A.1
The Investment Decision Triangle

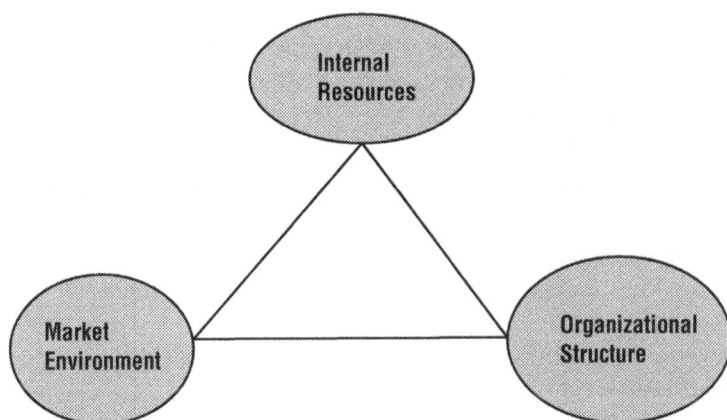

invest in the target market must assess how strong its internal resources are in relation to the expected challenges faced in the host market.

"Conditions relating to the market environment" refer to the pertinent "on-the-ground" conditions in the targetted markets. These would include wages and labour productivity, factor input supplies, physical infrastructure (including transportation and logistics), communications infrastructure, trade facilitation processes, local market demand, presence or absence of clusters of associated producers and suppliers, and, real and perceived social and cultural affinity between the investing firm and the host country. The firm in question must then question the extent to which these conditions can be exploited effectively in order to support the investment.

"Conditions relating to organizational structure" concern issues within the firm itself, and revolve around two key considerations — the transaction costs of producing overseas and the management of overseas production. The latter, the management of overseas production, is in turn affected by the industry and the product type(s) the firm is engaged in. Some product types such as garment and furniture manufacturing at one end of the spectrum and electronic parts at the other end, are easier for overseas production followed by reassembly in the home country or even in a third country. Other products such as those in the heavy industries and construction are less amenable to distributed production. Thus, the complexity of overseas production can challenge management capability depending on the nature of the industry and its inherent characteristics.

A decision to invest in a particular market has to, therefore, balance these three sets of considerations. At a highly generalized level, this process can be represented by the following chart.

The internal resources can be summarized as being either hard or soft. Hard resources are the technological and financial resources of the firm, whereas the soft resources are the firm's ability to access government assistance and build strong relations with the pertinent authorities and the like.

"Market environment" is also in turn summarized as two indicators. Cost advantages refer to whether the firm can exploit the lower wages and production costs of the target market, and whether the local infrastructure and logistics conditions are also cost-effective. Cultural advantage, on the

FIGURE A.2

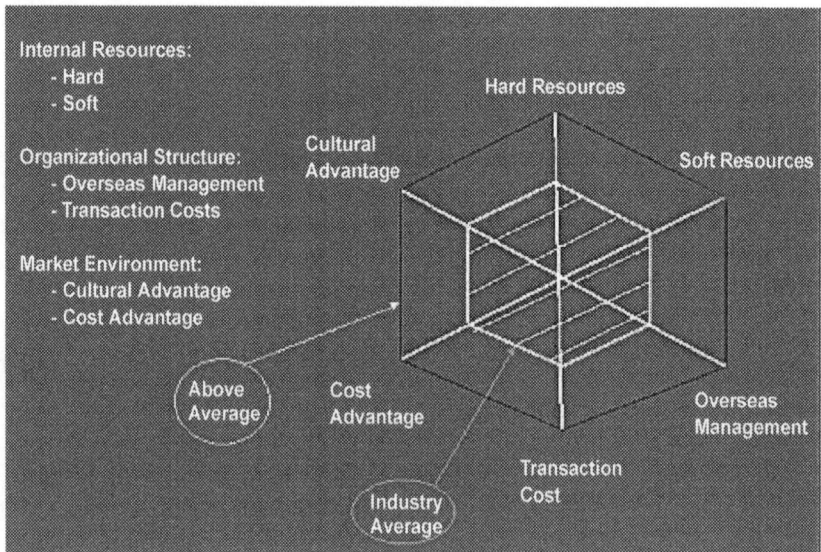

other hand, refers to whether the perceived cultural affinity (or the lack of) could be utilized to the firm's advantage.

"Organizational structure" considerations are condensed into the issues of transaction costs and overseas management. Transaction costs are cost differences related to having some production steps done overseas versus having them done in the home market. Different organizations could have different transaction costs depending on internal efficiency, structure and the processes prevalent within the firms. Overseas management refers to the strength of the management structure and its capabilities in coping with an overseas operation.

All these different nodes of the generalized framework are touched upon in the interview data obtained in this study. For example:

- Perceived strength in "soft resources" plus "cultural advantage" is meant to ease the overseas management challenges and reduce transaction costs, while facilitating the exploitation of the "cost advantage" of the host market. However, when the Chinese counterparts perceive that the strength of the Singapore firm is in its "hard resources", this gap in perceptions may actually increase the transaction costs, increase the burden of overseas management challenges, and reduce the effectiveness of the local cost advantage.
- The perceived "cultural advantage" therefore becomes a disadvantage because of a rigid management style that is incompatible with and unwilling to conform to local business practices. This disadvantage results in the erosion of some of the "soft resources" along with the local "cost advantage", and begins to tax "hard resources" further.

APPENDIX 3

OPERATING IN CHINA: ISSUES CASE STUDY 1
(IT COMPANY)

The IT industry has been growing rapidly in China. A Singapore firm was one of the main suppliers of intelligent building control technology when it first established a presence in China. As it became more involved in the market, it faced several challenges:

- *Regulatory restrictions.* The company had to seek a local partner because government regulations did not permit foreign companies to bid for contracts related to domestic construction projects.
- *Market risk sharing.* China's regional governments require large-sized projects to be split into many smaller ones to diversify the risks. This limits the scale of participation for the Singapore company which depends on scale for profitability.
- *Need for Singapore Government support.* In China, the government is usually responsible for the sourcing of large-scale infrastructure projects. The Singapore company sought and obtained the support of the Singapore general consul in Xiamen to contact officials of the Guangzhou government to facilitate its participation.
- *Handling power relations.* While construction projects in China are handled by the public sector, the success of a bid depends on effective communications between the decision-maker and bidder. This process involves rent-seeking, and payment of commissions. In some instances projects are channelled through specific agencies which are responsible for handling bidders. The Singapore company was seriously hampered in its attempts in dealing with the public sector in several of its early projects because of its inability to develop and nurture power relations.
- *Regional differences.* Different regions in China have different "rules of the game". In Beijing, for example, the middlemen believe in getting the cash upfront whether the business transaction succeeds or not. In Shanghai, on the other hand, the middlemen are expected to be compensated only after the contract is won. The Singapore company had to learn these regional differences over a long period of experience.

- *Financial restrictions.* Although the Singapore company learned the rules after a few years, it was prevented from some of these "extraneous" expenditures by the parent company in Singapore. This led to it being unable to compete with Chinese companies that brazenly obtained business, operating with flexibility by settling brokerages and commissions as needed.

APPENDIX 3

OPERATING IN CHINA: ISSUES CASE STUDY 2 (MANUFACTURING COMPANY)

This is joint-venture between a Singapore listed trading company and Chinese small valve manufacturer. The Singapore company was seeking a a manufacturing base in China, while the Chinese partner hoped to take advantage of preferential taxes, tax exemption for first three years followed by fifty-per cent tax reduction in the following two years. The Singapore partner put up the cash, while the Chinese partner provided the workshop, equipment and land.

- *No profits for six years.* In the first year all profits were distributed with nothing left for the company. For the following six years, the company had no profits because of rising material costs and intense competition.
- *Lack of strategic objective.* There was no long-term plan to develop the products or the market. The Singapore partner was a trading company with little knowledge of manufacturing, while the Chinese partner was a state-owned enterprise with no experience in market economics. This weakness allowed Taiwanese and other PRC companies to compete aggressively against it.
- *No core competency.* The product, valves, is low value added and material costs constitute 80 per cent of the cost of the product. Prices of valves have declined by 70 per cent but material costs have increased dramatically. Most of the employees are from the state-owned sector and have no cost efficiency yardsticks or understanding of product cost management.
- *Differences in cost control and lack of trust.* Singapore managers of the joint-venture spend most of their time on internal cost control while Chinese managers from the state-owned sector have little regard for cost control. Singapore managers insisted on documenting expense items for entertainment, which the Chinese managers found impossible to accept and considered to be an indication of a lack of trust.

- *Compensation gap.* Chinese managers from the state-owned sector could not understand why the Singapore general manager is paid $86,000 a year, while an ordinary employee's income is between $20,000 and 30,000, especially when the company is in the red.
- *Differences in corporate culture.* In Chinese SOEs, the labour union is considered part of the enterprise and union costs are borne by the enterprise. The Singapore general manager's view was that union activity was not part of the company's cost burden and was unwilling to support the union with company funds. This led to a decline in relationships between both parties with morale being eroded rapidly.

Index